FIND YOUR BEAT

Kirk House Publishers

FIND YOUR BEAT

WALK IN THE RHYTHM OF LIFE

TIM EGGEBRAATEN

Find Your Beat: Walk in the Rhythm of Life
Copyright © 2024 by Tim Eggebraaten

First Edition
Paperback ISBN: 978-1-959681-42-7
eBook ISBN: 978-1-959681-43-4
Hardcover ISBN: 978-1-959681-44-1
Library of Congress Control Number: 2024901552

Cover and Interior Design by Ann Aubitz

Published by Kirk House Publishers
1250 E 115th Street
Burnsville, MN 55337
Kirkhousepublishers.com
612-781-2815

This book is dedicated to:
My parents, Kenny and Pat Eggebraaten
My wife, Denise
Our three sons and the amazing women in their lives:
Josh and Mariah, Luke and Olivia, Isaac and Kyra
Our two grandsons, Kit and Wes
And to the men and women in Law Enforcement
I love you all!

FOREWORD

Tim Eggebraaten simply calls me "Coach." I call him "Chief." We have fondly spoken these words to one another over hundreds of calls, in-person sessions, partnering on stage, and exchanging stories and texts for the past thought-provoking seven years.

When this friendly, retired police chief entered my office with a guitar strapped over his shoulder, the "Chief" was like no one I had ever worked with. Within minutes, my intuition was proven accurate as he set his guitar down, smiled as big as a quarter moon, and said, "Coach, I'm all in! I feel called to carry out a positive message through songs and stories. I want to be giving with a purpose." And so, we began our deep dive using large storyboards surrounding the walls of my office. His thirst and commitment to learn the business of speaking created an atmosphere of boundless creativity between us. It was free flow, a brain dump on the walls that eventually became his brand of "Off Duty Chief." Those messy, handwritten, giant, sticky notes of unorganized thoughts, stories, and songs became the "Chief's" precious message that he would share with hundreds of audiences across the country.

One of Tim's signature stories includes a man named Norman, who changed his life. Tim has the amazing ability as a speaker and a writer to help us transform ourselves into seeing the Norman in all of us and the hope and strength we have for one another.

One of the biggest joys of coaching is seeing someone else's dreams transpire before my eyes as I watch the lightbulbs light up. It's incredible. Fireworks followed with excitement and self-realization for both of us. Not only did I see this humble, funny, good man find his way through the speaker world, but my job as a coach and business strategist was validated repeatedly. Isn't that the best when we can learn from one another?

As you read the pages of "Find Your Beat," you will quickly discover that it is a product of all who have left an indelible mark on *his* life. In those lessons learned, he shares with his audiences and you, the reader, the profound ability we have to make a difference in our everyday interactions.

His perspective and lack of ego were refreshing as I worked with him. He made me want to be a better person. I know you will enjoy the read that Tim has brought you in "Find Your Beat," and I hope you will get a chance to see him in person one day. He will surely upgrade your life, but he'll tell you that *you* did more for *him* than *he* did for *you*.

Renee' Wall Rongen – The "Chief's Coach"
Speaker, Author, Business Strategist
CEO – Renee Rongen & Associates, LLC
renee@reneerongen.com

TABLE OF CONTENTS

One	Stormin' Norman	11
Two	Lost the Beat	19
Three	Raised with Rhythm	25
Four	Best of Intentions	33
Five	The Big Change	43
Six	Struggling Along	53
Seven	Stand by Me	61
Eight	Awakening	71
Nine	One for the Road	77
Ten	Done with My Demon	87
Eleven	Road Trips with Dad	95
Twelve	Filter the Static	103
Thirteen	Letter Writing	109
Fourteen	Regaining My Rhythm	115
Fifteen	Take Your Shot	121
	Resources	127
	Acknowledgements	129
	About the Author	131

ONE
STORMIN' NORMAN

A welcome chill settled in one mid-summer evening in the northwestern Minnesota town of Detroit Lakes. I was a relatively new police officer in my mid-20s, smarter for the few years of experience I had logged working the night shift in the tourist town of 8,500 people that doubled in size during the summer. With the help of my previous employment as a security guard and correctional officer, some instructive mistakes, and the mentorship of senior officers, I was becoming a productive cop in our department of a dozen sworn officers and two civilian employees.

Detroit Lakes wasn't a hotbed of violent criminal activity. Nor was it quiet and gentle. Law-abiding people rarely knew what happened after they tucked into bed early.

During the first six years of my career, I worked relief shifts, covering for officers on vacation. Most were night shifts from 7:00 pm to 3:00 am. Those evening stints provided a wide variety of everything I had dreamed being a police officer would be. Foot chases, high-speed car pursuits, criminal investigations, arrests, interrogations, an occasional tussle, and a front-row seat to the greatest show on earth.

People from my hometown were always telling me, "You're too nice to be a cop." My parents, Kenny and Pat Eggebraaten of Fisher, Minnesota, were active and respected in our community of 413 inhabitants and modeled an immense optimism and work ethic for my three older sisters and me. The small town where I grew up was an extension of the goodness I felt at home. I love to say I ranked in the top 10 of my high school class of 1985 without disclosing I was one of only 18 graduates.

Growing up immersed in love and warmth taught me to seize and savor life. "This job won't change me," I told myself, "Tim Eggebraaten is going to change THE WORLD!" Early in my career as a police officer, however, my personality began to change. I was blind to it. With the steady diet of erratic shift work and dealing with people I believed would lie to me, try to fight me, or run from me, I was adopting an US-versus-THEM mindset.

"US" meant my partners and me on that night shift. I had their backs, and they had mine. "THEM" was almost everybody else. I started believing that defense attorneys and judges wanted to get our suspects off the hook by applying unrealistic laws and court procedures. Prosecutors refused to charge some of the bad guys because of so-called weaknesses in our case. Why would we have arrested the perps if they weren't guilty, right? Moreover, most civilians were part of THEM.

This mentality even crept into how I saw our department. At times, it seemed my police chief, captain, and sergeant had all forgotten what it was like to be a street cop—except on the occasions they made a decision that agreed with US. I was sure day shift officers loafed around the coffee pot while investigators played computer games and screwed up our perfect arrests with their lackluster effort to connect the dots and present a solid case to prosecutors.

US versus THEM permeated my thoughts, and I latched on to the feeling that almost everyone was against US. In my mind, my badge was bigger than life. Massive. I was a cop, and if you weren't, you had better do as I say.

This distrust and hyper-vigilance are common side effects of working as a police officer, says Dr. Kevin Gilmartin in his book *Emotional Survival for Law Enforcement*. I wasn't immune. The person I was becoming wasn't the Timmy Eggebraaten my family and friends knew back in Fisher. Timmy was a fun-loving, carefree kid who got along with everybody. My family and close friends began to see a personality change as the new Officer Eggebraaten persona spilled over into my life off-duty.

Off-duty? When was I ever off-duty? I was good at what I did, and I was always on. I could peer into dark streets and see people and objects moving several blocks away, all while driving, operating the police radio, and listening to classic rock on the dashboard FM. My senses were sharp, and I continued to hone my super kick-ass attitude.

So, on that cool summer night, when I got a radio call from the dispatcher, I was ready to thump and bump. The dispatcher—also an US-versus-THEM kind of guy—reported that a transient at the Holiday Inn needed a Salvation Army voucher for food or a place to stay. I grabbed my mic and told the dispatcher, "10-4. 638 is en route."

I had already decided I would give this guy minimal service so I could get back to real police work. Seriously—I was a cop in the *mean* streets of Detroit Lakes. I probably had two calls that night, but my mind was ramped up to chase murderers, rapists, and child molesters. The Chicago Police Department had nothing on the DLPD!

I arrived at the Holiday Inn and made my way inside, where I encountered the man in a spacious lobby that was decked in quintessential busy hotel carpet. He was mid-60s. Skinny. Gray hair. Brown eyes. By his left foot was a white plastic Walmart bag, which I surmised contained all his worldly possessions.

The man introduced himself to me as Norman James Lewis. He produced an identification card, and I "ran" him, radioing my dispatcher to check for outstanding warrants or other information. Norman's brown dress shoes and clothes led me to conclude he wasn't completely homeless or transient. And his eyes—something was different about his eyes.

When I asked Norman what was going on, he explained that he had boarded the bus in Minneapolis for Detroit, Michigan, to share an idea with automakers that would revolutionize car making. Detroit needed to hear his thoughts! Norman mentioned he had caddied for Tiger Woods and shared a few stories about his escapades.

On the bus to Detroit, Norman saw the sign for Detroit Lakes. I'm sure he was amazed at the brevity of the ride, and he got off the bus at Wal-Mart, about 900 miles shy of his original destination. He had nowhere to stay, not enough money to pay for a hotel room, and was a stranger in a town not even close to where he wanted to be. Norman lost his jacket when he left it in the Wal-Mart bathroom while washing his hands. A good Samaritan saw he was confused and gave Norman a ride to the Holiday Inn, where the desk clerk called the cops.

That's where I came in, a young police officer. Not only did I see the world as US versus THEM, but I believed only two types of people walked this earth: cops and suspects. I had grown a thick crust to protect me from getting hurt. I would not let myself get emotionally attached to others or let feelings interfere with my sworn job.

Norman was clearly a little confused. He wasn't a danger to himself or anyone else, but he was likely dealing with mental health challenges.

Norman was a kind, gentle man. And simply by being himself, he began to chip away at my protective crust. I asked him how I could help him on his journey. Norman hadn't done anything wrong, so I wasn't going to lock him up. I was sure my wife, Denise, would frown on me bringing a stranger home for her to watch for the evening.

Our department gave officers latitude to assess an individual's needs and issue a Salvation Army voucher to assist with a tank of fuel, a meal, or a hotel room for the evening. It allowed us to help someone down on their luck get to the next day, possibly to a larger community where they could find more assistance.

I escorted Norman to my squad car, where my K-9 partner, a 92-pound German Shepherd named Quincy, occupied most of the back seat. While there was enough room in a separate compartment in the back for my typical clients, Norman was different. I invited him to sit up front.

"Are you hungry?" I asked Norman. "Starving!" He exclaimed. We got to the office, where I grabbed the paperwork and a sack lunch prepared by jail kitchen staff—a sandwich, chips, and one of the best cookies in Northwest Minnesota. We returned to the car and drove to a different hotel that accepted vouchers.

As we arrived at the Castaway Hotel late this cool evening, I made a grand entrance with Norman and loudly introduced him to the lone night clerk in my best Monster Truck PA announcer voice. "I'd like you to meet 'Stormin' Norman.'" Norman continued to chip away at my crust as he giggled, humbly lowered his shoulders, and said, "Oh, no, I'm not Stormin'. I'm just Norman."

I signed the paperwork for the stay and bid them both farewell. As I was leaving, Norman said, "Wait a minute"! I stopped, and Norman looked at me. It wasn't a hasty glance. Norman locked onto me with his somehow special brown eyes. He wasn't looking *at* me but *into* me, down into my soul. His steady gaze was unlike anything I had ever experienced, and the few seconds Norman stared at me felt like minutes. Then he said, "I want to remember the people who have helped me." I just stood there, not knowing how to respond. I broke my gaze with him and told him to have a good night as I turned and shuffled out of the hotel.

I got into my squad car, radioed the dispatcher to report I had completed my call, leaned back into the seat, and cried.

I wasn't against crying, and I certainly don't see it as a sign of weakness, but at that stage of my life, I didn't cry. Unlike my current stage of life—retired cop, father, husband, and grandfather—who loses it watching Disney movies and live musicals.

But there I was. Mr. Badass Tough Cop sobbing in my patrol car while my loyal K-9 partner looked on. I asked myself, "Who have I become?"

This wasn't the Tim Eggebraaten raised by Pat and Kenny Eggebraaten in Fisher, Minnesota.

This wasn't the compassionate, caring boy who would go out of his way to help a family member, friend, or stranger.

Why did I get into police work? Wasn't it to help people?

All these emotions confronted me that cool night.

I got home that night around 3:30 AM and crawled into bed, still thinking about Norman. I rose early that morning, feeling like a jerk because I had a closet full of jackets, and Stormin' Norman didn't have even one. I grabbed a coat and headed out, looking for Norman.

He was already gone.

Norman J. Lewis "Gentle Spirit."

TWO

LOST THE BEAT

I couldn't shake the soul-piercing quality of my encounter with Norman. As the years piled on, my career progressed, and I faced the good and bad of police work, my emotional health had more ups and downs. Through it all, I thought often of Norman, a reverberating memory of a man who unexpectedly influenced my life.

As I began to write this book, my desire to learn more about Norman felt more pressing. In 2019, I performed music and delivered a keynote presentation for the National Association for Public Health Statistics and Information Systems (NAPHSIS) in Ohio. These public servants from around the country are charged with ensuring accurate and timely completion of birth and death certificates, along with other public health statistics.

I shared Norman's story during my presentation, and later, an association member approached me. "I think I can help you find Norman!" she said. I had avoided researching Norman's background because I wasn't sure what I would find, and I wanted nothing to alter my perception of him. This time, however, the thought of searching for him felt different. "That would be amazing," I responded. Within minutes, my new data expert friend found several public records about Norman James Lewis, born in 1936, including his date of death and burial at Fort Snelling National Cemetery. Norman was a Korean War Veteran.

A few weeks later, I made the over three-hour drive to Minneapolis for a meeting, and afterward, I drove to Fort Snelling Cemetery. I keyed Norman's name into a kiosk, which provided a reference number to find his grave. I opted against driving and began walking toward the section where Norman had been laid to rest. *It's a cemetery,* I thought. *How far could it be?*

Fort Snelling National Cemetery has interred more than a quarter million men and women of the armed forces across more than 400 acres, and my feet ached in my too-tight, non-arch-supporting black dress shoes. The closer I got to Section 31, Site 1647, the more my heart and pace quickened. I rounded a corner and half-sprinted to the white grave marker, a single slab in a sea of majestic rows paying tribute to our servicemen and women who had gone to their final resting place. "Here he is!" Looking closer at the headstone, I realized I was in the wrong section of the sprawling memorial park.

I reexamined the map, and once I got my bearings, I resumed my search. 1643, 1644, 1645, 1646… 1647. I found Norman J. Lewis – US Marine Corps, Korean War, March 27th, 1936 – April 4th, 2007! On the last line of the stone were inscribed the words "Gentle Spirit."

I wept and offered a brief prayer, thanking God for putting Norman into my life. After my moments with the man who so powerfully impacted me, I began a long, quiet walk back to my car.

In my search for Norman, I had spotted a man sitting alone among the endless white granite headstones. From a distance, his silhouette looked exactly like my dad, who had died just a year earlier. As I walked toward my car, the man was folding up an old nylon-webbed aluminum lawn chair. I felt drawn to walk over to him and start a conversation. Darwin was visiting his wife of "fifty years, three months, and five days." I was already an emotional wreck, and I listened to Darwin talk with a tear in his eye about losing the love of his life.

It was two strangers "randomly" meeting on a "random" day, except I believe there was nothing in our meeting that God didn't plan. Darwin needed to tell someone about his wife, and I needed to hear his story. His generation isn't known for dudes hugging each other, but I have become a hugger. I compromised and offered Darwin a side hug, one arm around his shoulder. As I leaned in, he began to cry.

"Hang in there, Darwin," was the best advice I could come up with on a moment's notice. My words fell far short of what I felt, but I hoped Darwin knew what our conversation meant to me. We went our separate ways, with deep emotions swirling in my head, heart, and gut as I continued my walk. I sent up another thank you to God for yet another person placed in my path.

I won't try to force you to believe what I believe. But I know more than ever that Stormin' Norman was a messenger sent by God to give me a swift yet lasting kick on the rear to help me remember my purpose.

We all encounter Normans and Normas—and Darwins and Darwinas—but we might not recognize their presence or their effect on us, whether in the moment or for the rest of our lives. Yet, when we intentionally open ourselves to these people, we can notice the powerful response they evoke in us. Moreover, we can see opportunities where we can impact others. With our words and actions, we each have the power to destroy someone's day or help them discover their destiny—who they are and why they matter in this world.

We can "Be the Norman"!

My first encounter with Norman when I was a relatively young police officer clearly hit a nerve within me. Our second graveside meeting—and my conversation with Darwin—confirmed an issue I had recognized over time and was working hard to put to rest. My problem? At many points in life, I had allowed circumstances and challenges to change me, and not always for the better.

I was off rhythm. I had lost my beat.

What do I mean by that?

Our lives are an intricate symphony of rhythm and harmony, weaving countless elements to create a beautiful song. Like in music, where various notes blend to form a melodic masterpiece, our lives are composed of diverse experiences, relationships, and responsibilities that harmoniously intertwine.

Rhythm permeates our daily existence, providing a steady beat that guides our actions and routines. Its pulse propels us forward, creating structure and momentum. From the typically predictable patterns of waking and sleeping to the cadence of work and leisure, rhythm shapes our lives and fills them with order.

Harmony represents the delicate balance and synchronization of various aspects of our lives. It's the art of blending our roles, goals, and dreams into a cohesive whole. Like the harmonious interplay of voices and instruments in our favorite song, all the parts of our lives—relationships, careers, hobbies, and physical, mental, and spiritual health—harmonize to form a symphony of fulfillment.

Achieving rhythm and harmony requires an awareness of our priorities and a conscious effort to synchronize the different elements. It involves recognizing when to focus on one area and when to shift attention to another, adapting to the ever-changing tempo of life. Life often requires us to improvise and adapt, just as musicians adjust their performance in response to the music around them.

Some days, the rhythm of our life is so strong we can't help but feel its pounding beat. Like when we feel good physically. Or we look forward to taking on whatever challenges might come our way. Or we have a social life where things move and groove. We can feel life's rhythm, and all its pieces are harmonious.

We also experience situations or seasons when we get offbeat. At times, we might readily identify what skews our rhythm. It might be an argument with a loved one or friend. Or uncertainty regarding health or career. Or perhaps we can't pinpoint the source, but something is making our rhythm misfire. We feel off-pitch, and the harmony of life is out of tune.

No matter who we are, each day invites us to find our beat, to walk in the rhythm of life.

For almost three decades in criminal justice, I witnessed true heroes in action—police officers, firefighters, EMS personnel, doctors, nurses, farmers, teachers, and others—people who did the right things for the right reasons. They set aside their fears of being harmed and helped others.

During all those years, I also watched people do unspeakable things to children, adults, senior citizens, and themselves. I looked evil in the face and saw that evil indeed does exist. I realized the world needs people to step up to disrupt it and hold violators accountable for their actions.

Despite that constant grinding negativity, I'm at a stage of life, at least for today, where I am physically, mentally, and spiritually healthy. I can feel my rhythm of life, and all the parts of life are in harmony.

I know the rhythm and harmony are real, and I'll do anything to find my beat. Tomorrow, I may wake up and recognize my rhythm is off. I would have been lost in knowing how to respond at one point. Now I know what to do. I can apply the tactics I share in this book to regain and retain my rhythm.

This book contains life lessons taught by my parents, bosses, mentors, friends, and strangers that I have applied to succeed against the challenges of a law enforcement career and significant life events. These tactics will help you and me work on our attitudes and improve our Rhythm of Life. Honestly, they are simple. That doesn't equate to being easy. As with all new behaviors, creating positive and healthy habits requires focus, encouragement from others, practice, patience, and dedication. But I can tell you that the results you will receive are a hundred percent worth the effort you put into achieving them.

Whatever your goals—relationship strengthening, career aspirations, weight loss, stress reduction, financial independence, stepping into a new phase of life—the only way to reach them is to develop a plan and consistently work with it.

Take the stories and tactics of this book as a personal challenge. By applying the techniques in the following pages, you will see positive results in your overall attitude that make you better friends, partners, spouses, parents, leaders, and employees. More importantly, we see the world more positively when we turn these techniques into habits. These lessons have changed my life; I hope you will allow them to help change yours.

THREE
RAISED WITH RHYTHM

Mom and Dad always said I was whistling before I could talk. "A whistling kid is a happy kid," they would say. Music was infused into my life, and some of my earliest childhood memories include rhythm and harmony.

When I was 12 years old, I attended one of many biennial Eggebraaten family reunions at my aunt and uncle's home near Bemidji, Minnesota, just miles from the headwaters of the Mississippi River. With 13 children in my dad's family, and each child having multiple children and grandchildren, over 100 Eggebraatens wandered the Northwoods that weekend, connecting with each other, sharing memories, and creating new moments.

Music was a massive part of my dad's family as they grew up in the 1930s, 40s, and 50s. Dad had a decent singing voice but often told me, "The world needs listeners, too, Timbob! We can't all be good singers!" Several of my aunts would have been shoo-ins for today's *American Idol* or *The Voice* singing competitions. They sang Sweet Adeline harmonies, and my dad and his brothers crooned intricate barbershop tunes.

Many at the reunion were exceptional musicians. As the activities rolled into the evening, tight harmonies and laughter mixed with the occasional magical cry from the Minnesota State Bird, the Loon. My grandma and grandpa, Helga and Arthur, sat in their wheelchairs by the roaring bonfire, snug in their lap blankets made by my grandma, with flames reflecting off their glasses and smiles beaming on their faces. We sang old hymns, folk songs, and hits from back in the day. Grandma sometimes offered up a song in the beautiful Norwegian language. It was magical.

When I belted out "The Duke of Earl" in my new-found falsetto voice, I gained confidence and relished the reaction I received from my aunts and a few cousins. But everything blurred into faint background sights and sounds when my oldest cousin, Ellis, started on his acoustic guitar. As the bonfire flames flickered, embers crackled, and smoke rose into the clear Minnesota skies, Ellis cranked out "House of the Rising Sun" by Eric Burton and the Animals. At that moment, my mission became clear. I would communicate through rhythm and harmony for the rest of my life. I would someday learn to play the guitar, and that song would become one of my signature pieces. When people ask me now, "Tim, what's your favorite song?" "House of the Rising Sun" is shelved in the top five!

I finally found a way to start playing guitar in my sophomore year in college. As a Resident Assistant (RA) at Minnesota State University in Moorhead, I got to know most of the guys on my all-male dorm floor, First East Ballard Hall. Nathan and Roger (a.k.a. Butch) lived directly across the hall from me. Nate was a clean-cut kid with short brown hair swooped to the side who used words like "shucks," "darn," and, when he was really mad, "crap!" Butch was skinny and rocked a mullet that touched his shoulders. Nathan wore plaid button-up shirts, while Roger's wardrobe consisted of black Metallica and Def Leppard t-shirts.

These two guys didn't know each other before the school year began, but they quickly discovered they were both proficient guitar players. True to their personalities, Nate played country, bluegrass, and 1950s and 60s tunes, while Butch cranked out AC/DC licks with distortion and reverb in their DNA.

I owned a cheap Fender acoustic guitar, and I yearned to play like Nate and Butch. One day, as I struggled to find three chords and answer the ageless college question of "What is truth," Nate asked me what kind of music I liked. I told him I was partial to music from the 50s and 60s. I demonstrated my G, C, and D chords, and he unveiled the E-minor chord. "What the hell did you just do?" I looked at him with bewilderment. "Do that again!" My world changed when he combined the G, E-minor, C, and D chords. That chord progression triggered a thousand of my favorite songs to flood my senses at once. "Wait until you hear A-minor," Nate teased. MIND = BLOWN!

The entire purpose of a college education and a degree in Criminal Justice shriveled nearly to extinction that day. Instead of my daily trips to the classes designed to get me a B.A. (that's Bachelor of Arts, not "Bad Attitude") degree, I prioritized building calluses on my left-hand fingertips.

Much to the pained dismay of my floormates, I practiced Del Shannon's "Runaway" incessantly. My guitar accompanied me as I made regular RA rounds through the dorm, ensuring all was quiet and on visits to the front desks of other dorms. I could prop open my guitar case like a busker for hours, but the notorious cheapness of college students meant I received few monetary gratuities. Instead, my guitar case filled up with individual packets of ketchup, mustard, and saltine crackers, with just an occasional nickel or dime. I imagined Johnny Cash had a similar start to his career.

Nowadays, a song seems to always be in my head, whether I sing in the shower, belt out a tune as I drive, or melodically answer questions from my grown children. "Dad, not everything has to be a song," explained one of my boys as I sang to him. Enter 12-bar blues riff: "You're telling me (ba-dah-dah-dah-dum), I don't need to sing (ba-dah-dah-dah-dum), well, let me tell you son (ba-dah-dah-dah-dum), you might not know everything!" Grab the broom for the wailing guitar solo and wait for the obligatory eye roll right before the kid walks away, shaking his head.

Music means a lot to me. Yet, as I grew up, rhythm and harmony meant even more than a literal beat, tune, or accompaniment. It's about life itself—how we live, what we stand for, and how everything holds together.

An irrepressible rhythm of life ran through my family.

Mom and Dad Eggebraaten

I'll start with my mom—Patricia Halos Eggebraaten, Pat, Patsy Jean, Boom Boom Grandma—was an expert at speaking and demonstrating how to live with rhythm. She walked the talk. She needed to wear shoes to break five feet tall, but she gave the impression she stood six or seven feet as she voiced a phrase that still rings inside me: "I Am, I Can, I WILL!"

In the mid-1970s, I helped Mom study for the United States Postal Service Exam in her bid to be the first female Postmaster in Fisher, Minnesota, ZIP Code 56723. As a pre-teen, I began learning about analogies, proper grammar, punctuation, math problems, and multiple other topics as I quizzed her in preparation for her written assessment. Countless times as she studied, she paused and uttered, "I Am, I Can, I WILL!" I couldn't help but internalize the phrase because she repeated it so many times. I began to take on her mindset and believed I had complete control over my attitude, even if the events around me were outside my control.

Mom crushed the test and was appointed Postmaster for Fisher. Many called her "Postmistress," a term she didn't love. "I'm nobody's mistress!" she would say with disgust. She held the position until her retirement in 2001.

Mom became an institution in our tiny community as she did far more than sorting mail. She delivered hope and love to the people who needed it most. Mom had the ability to read people and instantly understood what they lacked in their lives. In her role at the post office, she served abused, poverty-stricken, rich, shy, and boisterous people. Somehow, she stripped the disguise human beings can wear and got down to what made them tick. She used her powers to listen to those who needed to talk or hug those who had difficulty believing love was real. Without any psychological training, social media, or even an electric typewriter, this compact giant had an unimaginable impact on everybody she encountered. She taught others how to be a difference-maker. Even years after she died in 2016, people still tell me how she made them feel when they went to the post office to get their mail. Some describe it as the highlight of their day. What a legacy!

What does the rhythm in your life feel like? Where does it come from? Does the collection of beats come from the people you spend time with—your family, friends, co-workers, or peers?

I haven't invented any of the tactics discussed in this book. Still, I have had the blessings of role models throughout my life—parents, supervisors, teachers, bosses, friends, and mentors who have provided living examples of the power of these techniques.

I was raised with an irrepressible rhythm, which I sum up as positivity. *Stay in the Groove and Make Positive Thinking a HABIT, starting right now!* **is the first tactic we all need to bring to life.**

But is it possible to make a habit of positive thinking? Doesn't it get more challenging the more we become set in our ways? It's easy to say, "This is just who I am, and I can't change that."

Positivity can indeed feel difficult as we get older—or if we feel like life has broken us and forced us to become people we don't want to be. Yet psychologists studying positivity tell us that 40 to 60 percent of our personalities are malleable. In other words, we can effectively change much of who we are by being intentional and applying effective techniques. Yes, our genetics and environment are crucial for developing our attitudes and personalities, but we can't ignore our ability to change.

My dad was Superman to me. In his prime, he was 6 foot 2 inches, with 225 pounds of muscle, and he tossed hundred-pound potato sacks like bags of potato chips. He seemed impervious to pain and always had fresh scrapes and scabs on his hands from brushes with sharp objects. The fact that he retained all ten of his digits throughout his life was miraculous. He worked nights and weekends early in his 40-year career as a communications agent with the Burlington Northern Railroad. He slept during the day while I occupied my time quietly playing with my toys. Whether it was my Evel Knievel motorcycle and action figure (not a doll!) getting ready to launch over the Grand Canyon (that is, the couch) or The Six Million Dollar Man Steve Austin (also not a doll!) rescuing Malibu Barbie and her friends (those were dolls, but they belonged to my sisters!) from certain death, I had to ensure the screams didn't wake my dad.

Despite his erratic work schedule, Dad always found time to participate actively in our lives. Even in our basement adventures, as Evel Knievel somehow decided to jump through a fiery circle of death and flames from the burning toilet paper left their impression on the burgundy 1970s carpet, Dad rarely responded with anger. He embodied everything good about a gentle giant that you can imagine.

Dad got physical with me only once. I had ignored his repeated requests for help raking leaves in the backyard. Tinkering with my motorcycle spark plugs took precedence over his need for assistance. After his third and apparently final request, Dad came into the garage, grabbed my arm, which was attached to my 150-pound frame, and gave me a shake. As far as shakes go, this one wouldn't knock an egg off a spoon, but the message intertwined with that rapid movement was undeniable. Dad was pissed, and he had reached a point where he felt words were no longer enough to relay his thoughts. Years later, he told me that he witnessed his father, Arthur, lose control and spank one of my uncles so hard that my uncle nearly passed out. I have no doubt Dad feared the rage possibly residing in his genes and remained alert to incidents provoking this potential response.

Dad continued to maintain an optimistic outlook on life. He and my mom were skilled at examining life events with a twist of positivity. As a kid, I sometimes wished they would wallow with me in my bouts of self-pity, but they always responded with a

"Well, it could be worse" or "Look on the bright side," followed by a skilled analysis that had become automatic for them.

Mom had mastered one fundamental form of positivity: gratitude. She regularly transformed a mundane activity into greatness by saying, "This is the best bottle of water I've ever had at a South Dakota rest area in August with my son!" Or "I don't remember a more beautiful sunrise on Saturday, May 14th, 1989!"

Gratitude is one of the most potent and accessible exercises we can do daily to practice positivity. Dr. Martin Seligman, often called the Father of Positive Psychology, has done massive research into the effects of gratitude. One study involved documenting three to five aspects you are thankful for daily and exploring how they make you feel and impact your life. I take it a step further and review the list when I wake up. That "attitude of gratitude" gives me a mental and spiritual boost I can carry with me through the day.

These lists can be as simple as a notebook by your bed or electronic apps. I have downloaded and experimented with a dozen "Gratitude Apps" on my phone. Many are free and include daily notifications asking, "What are you thankful for?" The reminders always seem to pop up at the perfect time, as I'm getting frustrated with a challenge in my daily routine. When we focus on what we're thankful for, the issues throwing a wrench into our day become less significant.

When we develop a habit of looking for the pieces of our lives we're thankful for and then giving thanks to our Creator or to a person responsible for that piece, our brains begin to see good things everywhere.

FOUR
BEST OF INTENTIONS

As long as I can remember, I wanted to be a cop. My parents, Kenny and Pat Eggebraaten of the Northwest Minnesota town of Fisher raised four children. They cranked out three daughters before they got it right and had me, their favorite son. Mom and Dad taught us to be caring, thoughtful, and conscientious people, so as I followed my dream of becoming a police officer, my whole head and heart were dominated by a desire to help people. I was going to make a difference.

My thoughts of policing go back at least as far as kindergarten when I pondered all the good things an officer does to assist everyday people. When I was seven, we took a family trip to Seattle to see my mom's Aunt Clara. On her end table, I spotted a picture of a man in the Washington State Police uniform. He was Aunt Clara's son, Roger, making him my mom's first cousin. Dang, that uniform! The Smokey Bear hat, crisp laser-straight shirt creases, and a shiny badge. He looked like a strong, brave hero, and I *knew* someday I would be a police officer.

For a brief time in junior high, I flirted with the goal of becoming a lawyer, but I dropped that nonsense when I found out how much a lawyer needs to read. Reading was 83rd on my list of enjoyable activities.

I had to wait until my junior year of college to experience what I dreamed about for so long. I signed up for a ten-week internship with the Fargo, North Dakota, Police Department, a few incredibly flat miles from my university in Moorhead, Minnesota. As I rotated through each division within the department, the 40 unpaid hours a week were my first real exposure to the day-to-day life of a licensed police officer.

No intern anywhere ever ranks high among actual paid employees, a reality that unquestionably holds true among cops. The experienced officers weren't cruel to me. They just didn't care to bond with some punk guaranteed to be gone in a few weeks. It didn't help that a previous intern had written a blistering letter to the local newspaper disagreeing with a Fargo officer's actions on a case. Understandably, trust was lacking between officers and the wannabees embedded in their ranks. I got it. My duty as an intern was to observe, learn, speak when spoken to, and stay out of the way.

My first day of a two-week stint with the Detective Bureau was marked by a murder investigation of a man shot under a bridge over the winding Red River splitting North Dakota and Minnesota, where bridges created shelters for homeless people and cover for drug deals.

To keep me out of their way, the detectives assigned me the menial task of organizing pawn shop receipts in alphabetical order by the name of the person purchasing or pawning an item. That didn't mean I was completely shut out from their work. As they huddled a few feet away from me, discussing the murder, I overheard them mention a potential suspect.

The suspect's name triggered a snapshot in my brain from filing the pawn receipts a couple of days earlier. I quietly went over to *my* file cabinet, slyly slid open *my* drawer, and casually thumbed through *my* receipts until I found the name the detectives had mentioned. "HOLY CRAP!" The receipt showed *our* suspect had purchased a handgun from a local pawn shop only a few weeks prior to the killing. Could this be the murder weapon?!?

My body shook as I approached the small group of senior detectives to show them the document that could blow the case wide open. "Ahem." I cleared my throat. "Did I hear you say 'Ralph' was a suspect in *our* homicide?" Yes, I took ownership as if I were an indispensable, permanent part of the team. "Here's a pawn slip showing he bought a gun."

The pubescent squeak in my voice didn't bolster my credibility, and I admit I expected them to hoist me onto their shoulders and parade me around the police department as they sang my praises. I pictured Lieutenant Cal Eggers recommending me to the chief, who would indeed offer me a job on the spot. Instead, the detectives grabbed the paper without a word and began chasing that fresh lead. I quickly realized I wouldn't receive their acknowledgment or thanks, but I was feeling a freaking adrenaline rush like nothing I had experienced before. I had connected the dots in an active murder investigation while carrying out the mundane task of alphabetizing pawn slips. It was exhilarating. I made a difference!

For this future crime fighter, the men and women of the Fargo Police Department proved to be outstanding examples of professional cops. I was able to hold my college career together and graduated in 1989 with a Criminal Justice Degree after four years at MSU. Neighboring college and MSU rival Concordia College hired me as a security guard right after graduation, and the Clay County Jail also brought me on as a correctional officer. Both jobs would help shape the psyche I needed to be a good cop.

Besides graduating and scoring two great jobs, I made the best decision of my life and married Denise in June of that year. For two years, I hammered away at both jobs. Both employers required me to wear brown polyester uniform pants. Unfortunately, I couldn't do anything to make them less ugly. While I couldn't afford to get them altered, I used a trick I learned from my mom. I rolled up the legs and stapled them in place to get the right length. A quick hit of a brown marker on the staples made them nearly invisible (follow me for more fashion ideas)!

For two years, I learned how to sleep even when I wasn't tired because I wasn't sure when I would get to sleep again. Both schedules were erratic, as both places considered me part-time. At the jail, however, "part-time" meant at least 40 hours a week covering shifts when full-timers were on vacation or sick.

Especially the first year, there were many times I worked eight hours at the jail, reported to the college for an eight-hour shift, had 16 hours off, then eight hours at the jail, then eight hours off—the chaos went on and on. Sometimes, I forced myself to sleep after only nine hours awake because, in eight more hours, I would pull a jail shift followed by another school shift. Three times that summer, I worked 24 hours straight.

All this work cut into my guitar practice, so I occasionally brought my guitar to the jail to pick and grin in the control room. One of my partners, Steve, also played. To help the shifts go faster, we made up ridiculous songs about our coworkers and life.

I met some incredible, bigger-than-life cops at the Moorhead Police Department who became my friends and mentors. "Ask, Tell, Make" was a common practice among them as they interacted with the public. One officer explained to me, "Tim, if I'm talking to someone and I want them to take their hands out of their pockets,

- I will ASK them to please take their hands out so I can see them. If they don't immediately comply,
- I will TELL them to show me their hands. If they still don't comply, it's time to go 'hands-on' and
- MAKE them take their hands out of their pockets."

The officers I learned from in those formative years of my career were tough, compassionate, intelligent, and dedicated to serving others. They were the real deal!

I got my first real police officer opportunity when Chief Walter J. Tollefson from Detroit Lakes, Minnesota, offered me a job that would begin on July 1st, 1992. Chief Tollefson was a calm man who had "been there, done that," and he reminded his officers we could make very few mistakes he hadn't already made. His main requests to us were to be honest with him and to own our actions. He would be one of several exemplary bosses I was blessed to learn from.

Detroit Lakes wasn't even on my radar for submitting my applications to be a police officer because, after college, I grabbed my Minnesota road map and circled the cities in the state with populations greater than 30,000. Detroit Lakes had only 8,500. But Detroit Lakes also had 412 gorgeous lakes within a 25-mile radius, and it was only 50 minutes from Moorhead—the home of my dream police department.

Detroit Lakes Police Captain Ed Schmidt noticed my resumé said I could speak Spanish. "We have a company in town that employs many people whose primary language is Spanish," he said, "and it would be beneficial to communicate with them if we had someone who could speak their language."

"Si, hablo un pocito Español!" I replied.

Captain Schmidt and Chief Tollefson had no clue what I had just said, but they were impressed enough to hire me. I knew enough Spanish phrases to have a rudimentary conversation and to tell them to put their hands up or spread their buttocks with their hands—you know, the practical verbiage you could repeat at your favorite Mexican restaurant if you wanted to get concerned looks from the staff—but it certainly wasn't enough to make me an actual translator.

When Chief Tollefson offered me the job, he suggested, "Ya know, a lot of the officers who start here finish their careers here. There's a high probability you'll call this place home and retire with the Detroit Lakes Police Department!"

Yeah, right! I thought. *I'll work here for a year, get some experience, and apply for the Moorhead PD!* "Yes, sir!" I acknowledged while winking to myself, believing full well I would give the DLPD 12 months of my life.

A couple of weeks before my official first day, I had driven from our apartment in Fargo to Detroit Lakes to sign employment papers for the city's Human Resource Department, and Chief Tollefson asked if I wanted to stick around and help with a narcotics search warrant or go back home to my apartment. He didn't have to ask twice.

The Chief and several plain-clothes narcotics investigators entered the tiny home on West Front Street through the front door, and I brought up the rear. Caught up in my excitement, I didn't realize that they all had their guns out until we were inside. I was wearing jeans and a T-shirt, and I didn't even have a pencil to protect me. After we searched the house for bad guys and found no one at home, we got down to the gritty execution of a narcotics search warrant.

The house had a cellar with a trap door on the kitchen floor that led to the lair of an aspiring horticulturist, with a system of fluorescent lights blazing down on hundreds of marijuana plants. My new partners seized the opportunity to harness my enthusiasm and tasked me with counting each plant and helping them document and seize them. While it wasn't the adrenaline-pumping adventure I had experienced vicariously watching countless episodes of COPS, honestly, they could have ordered me to roll in dog pooh, and I still would have been on top of the world.

On the evening of my first official shift as a licensed peace officer—a real COP—I walked three blocks from our blue rental house on Oak Street in my new, freshly polished black "cop" boots. I was dressed in dark navy pants, a spotless light blue polyester shirt with navy blue epaulets, wearing a shiny DLPD Patrol Officer badge, pristine leather duty belt and holster, my .357 revolver, two speed loaders with six bullets each, radio, and the handcuffs I had purchased during my eight weeks of skills training in Hibbing. I sported a fresh haircut and an obligatory 90s cop mustache, neatly trimmed. The whole shebang!

As I reached for the back door of the Detroit Lakes Police Department, an overstuffed keyring jingled in my trembling hand. Years of visualizing this moment flashed through my head like an old film projector displaying memories onto a wall. I had wanted to be a cop forever, and here I was, ready to embark on my career.

To the outside world, it was easy to identify me as a police officer. Along with having the appearance of a peace officer came a biased assumption this guy had all the answers. He's highly trained and able to take on a dozen ninja warriors twice his size without excessive force. He's a marksman, negotiator, legal expert, psychiatrist, therapist, and a human being full of compassion. This cop obviously has the resources to take a microscopic speck of paint from a car bumper and locate the individual who committed a hit-and-run in the Wal-Mart parking lot. He's just like everyone's favorite TV cop, solving the most complicated crimes in 60 minutes.

The world couldn't see the inexperienced young man who was giddy to have landed his dream job. The man who had been married for three years and would be a new father in a month. The boy who grew up spending thirteen years of elementary, junior high, and senior high school in the Northwest Minnesota town of Fisher, four years of college and a bachelor's degree in criminal justice from MSU, and eight weeks of law enforcement skill training in Hibbing to gain some of the knowledge base necessary to be a cop. His three years as a security guard and correctional officer would remove some of the naivete from growing up in a tiny town of 413. Some of it, anyway.

As I tried to get the correct key into the lock, my heart thumped like the kick drum at a sold-out Metallica concert. As I fiddled with the doorknob, the door opened from the inside. Standing in the doorway was Dick, the veteran officer I was replacing. It was his last shift, and we had never met before this moment. His worn leather gear, unpolished badge, and less-than-tidy uniform contrasted starkly with my equipment. He looked tired. Dick studied me with the experience of decades of dealing with people during their worst moments and an amazing ability to read people.

"Are you my replacement?" he grumbled. I felt like the two-month-old puppy that wanted to play with the old, white-muzzled hound while biting his ears and pouncing on his back. I couldn't contain my exuberance when I replied, "Y-y-yes!" He stared at me and said, "Well, you can have it!" He pushed past me, got into his car, and drove away, leaving me standing there with my mouth wide open and wondering what I had just gotten myself into.

I didn't know Dick well enough to accurately assess how he felt about law enforcement, his co-workers, the citizens, or his supervisors. Still, he gave me the impression that he'd had enough and wouldn't miss any of it in his retirement.

I immediately made a vow to myself:

- I would NOT leave this career angry and bitter with people!
- This job and whatever the world threw at me would NOT change me. No way!
- Tim Eggebraaten from Fisher, Minnesota, was determined to change THE WORLD!

FIVE
THE BIG CHANGE

An urban legend suggests that *Playboy* magazine once listed the Detroit Lakes City Beach as a top ten beach in the United States. I haven't seen the article, and I'm not convinced it exists. The tale, however, lured tens of thousands of young people to our beautiful lakes country every July 4th weekend during the late 1980s and early '90s. The resort town of 8,500 people swelled to more than 20,000 as visitors came to party, watch the fireworks, and possibly meet the man or woman of their dreams.

As I launched into my job with the Detroit Lakes Police Department, Captain Schmidt did his best to boost my confidence. "Well, you're no newbie!" he said. Sure, I was 25—a little older than the average new cop—and had worked as a correctional officer for a whopping three years. I still felt like a fish out of water. I was an excited fish, nonetheless.

On my first shift as a sworn police officer, I was partnered with Sgt. Paul Goecke. Right out of the chute, he designated me as the squad car driver. Everything was new to me! I had never even driven a Chevrolet Caprice, so I had to learn to apply my foot to the brake to get the car in gear. Paul pointed me west of town out on U.S. Highway 10 and encouraged me to play with the lights and siren. First, to get the urge out of my system. Second, to settle my nerves. Third, to begin to master the squad's dozens of buttons and switches.

After a few hours of cruising around, we arrested a female drunk driver and cited a young guy with illegal fireworks. With that experience, I got the green light from Sgt. Goecke to explore the town by myself.

I drove a few blocks and saw a teenager vandalizing a public bathroom. Instinct told me to chase the little turd, so I hopped out of my car and started running. He tossed the recently ripped-off paper towel dispenser and bolted. I was a high school and college sprinter, but 30 pounds of leather, gun, bullets, and bullet-proof vest slowed me down. Moreover, the youngster ran faster scared than I could run mad.

When the delinquent eluded me, I had no clue how to describe my location. I had been to Detroit Lakes only a handful of times just to test and interview for the job. I didn't yet know street names or landmarks. Radioing my situation would have been futile, not to mention embarrassing.

On my second shift, I was assigned a cadet from Alexandria Technical College as my partner. This poor guy read the map and feverishly shouted turn-by-turn instructions while I responded to help Ozzy, a deputy sheriff, who had pulled over a suspected stolen car. I wonder what the cadet thought of the rookie cop assigned as his "mentor." I'm thankful nobody got hurt because of me. I quickly learned to study more experienced officers and adapt.

On the Fourth of July, with three shifts under my belt, I was assigned to foot patrol with Burt, a different cadet partner. Burt and I hitched a ride to the beach from one of our senior officers, John Bellefeuille. Burt took the "shotgun" seat, relegating me to the back. I was starting to feel the confidence of a seasoned veteran, so I didn't mind. It was better than hoofing it.

A minute into the ride, the voice of another officer screamed out of the radio, reporting his intent to stop a black Firebird Trans Am, but the driver kept rolling. "Northbound on Summit! Northbound on Summit!" came the high-pitched voice over the radio. The foot patrol officer was trying to outpace the muscle car, which made for a short chase! We soon intercepted the Trans Am, prompting John to pull a U-turn, hit the lights, and make chase. With each sharp turn, I ping-ponged from door to door along the back seat.

John nearly called off the pursuit, assessing the potential danger to crowds already in town to enjoy the party atmosphere and impressive fireworks show. Then the Trans Am guy turned left onto a dead-end street. We had him!

John and Burt bolted from the car to make the apprehension. I grabbed my .357 revolver from the holster and yanked the door handle to extricate myself from the back seat and help take the bad guy into custody—momentarily forgetting I was in the rear seat of a police car. With the door handles disabled to prevent escape, I was locked in with nothing to do but rap my revolver barrel on the window as cops ran past me to join the party. Ted, a state trooper, finally gave me my freedom. Calmly, he added, "Son, holster your gun."

Just days into the job, I was already hooked on adrenaline, the physical and mental rush this career would supply me over the next two and a half decades. My badge felt huge with power and authority. But anyone with law enforcement or military experience—or a shred of common sense—could see my tactics needed work.

Later that night, I saw John on the beach, standing at ease, smoking a cigarette, and waiting for the fireworks to start. "That was INTENSE!" I said, referring to our chase. "Yeah, I guess it was pretty crazy," John responded casually as he took a long drag from his smoke. What the hell? Does this guy have ice water in his veins? How can he be so calm after the most exhilarating ride ever?

Arriving in my long-anticipated career—plus experiencing the birth of our first of three sons, Joshua, about a month after my start in Detroit Lakes—put me on top of the world. My erratic shifts meant Denise and I had little need for daycare in those early years. I covered Daddy Dayshift, meaning doing fun things with Josh, like going to the park, making lunch, and playing Hot Wheels. I handed off our little man to Denise and went to my job while she did the far more challenging work of bathing and bedtime preparation.

It was a magical season of my life. But I had started to change.

Back then, a retired Detroit Lakes Police Sergeant, Leroy "Gundy" Gunderson, told me I would encounter events "you can't make up" and suggested I write my thoughts. "You'll be able to write a book," he said. Journaling didn't stick as an everyday habit, though it resurfaced throughout my career. I did, however, keep almost all my pocket notebooks, and perusing them now elicits smells, images, and sounds as if I had jetted back in time and was witnessing events again, this time as a third party. A suspect's scribbled name or a victim's name and address triggers a flood of memories.

I now can see a metamorphosis when I go through my off-and-on journal and the scrapbook I assembled of newspaper clippings from my early years on the force. As I view my stories through the eyes of a retired cop and chief—not to mention a grandpa and a man who has practiced mindfulness and meditation for a few years, whose stress level rarely approaches level two out of ten—a shift in tone is clear.

I see now what I didn't see then. I sometimes put down the journal out of embarrassment about who I was at the time. What did my parents think about my mutating personality? What transformations did my wife notice? At my core, had I become as big of a jerk as the guy on those pages, or was I just a product of my environment? Does everybody undergo changes like this?

Granted, a police officer on a traffic stop or chasing a suspect doesn't have the luxury of assuming a person means the officer no harm. At that time and place, it really is us-versus-them. Uniformed officers donning riot helmets, shields, and batons, holding a line to protect people or property while being buffeted with rocks, spit, and insults, are in every literal sense in an us-versus-them situation.

The challenge lies in controlling that feeling. It's not an easy emotion to turn on and off. For all of us, politics and global events in the age of social media have fueled the divisiveness of us-versus-them. Hiding behind a keyboard makes it easy to hurl hateful epithets toward strangers, and the anonymous back-and-forth further fuels hatred and fear. It's easy to label people. We come up with words and phrases to lump others together by their race, religion, physical characteristics, gender, and sexual preference. These descriptors can be vile and hateful, readily weaponized to cause pain.

Only when we quiet our rhetoric and endeavor to humanize people can we begin to understand each other. It's much easier to talk about "the 'illegals' bringing their drugs into our country and raping our women," for example, than it is to see and treat people as individuals who may be looking for a better and safer way of life for themselves and their families. The one-sided narratives we listen to can drown out reality. It takes effort to train our minds to think objectively and rationally.

If I had an opportunity to talk sense to my younger self, I don't know if I could have shifted my thinking. I was in high gear. I was locked into us-versus-them. By the year 2000, I was a patrol sergeant working primarily from 7 pm to 3 am. My constant companion was Quincy, my K-9 partner. My ability to read people, as sharp as it would ever be, was accompanied by a ramped-up sense of duty to clean up our community by confronting thieves, drug dealers, and violent offenders.

In those days, our young, fearless, and driven night crew shared a passion for aggressive, proactive law enforcement. Together with our brothers and sisters from the Becker County Sheriff's Office, the Minnesota State Patrol, the Department of Natural Resources, and other state and federal agencies, we collaborated like a precision machine to enforce the law and make our community safe for everyone.

The strong sense of teamwork among agencies fluctuated throughout the years, but at that time, we didn't pay attention to the color of our uniforms. We all played from the same sheet of music.

So, when we received multiple complaints from good citizens about suspicious, potential narcotics activities in a specific house, we paid attention. I took the complaints to Patrick, the Drug Task Force officer at the sheriff's office, but I got the impression this house wasn't a high priority. I was surprised. Pat was always a bloodhound on a fresh scent, following up on narcotics leads. "Oh well!" I told myself. "If Pat won't get involved, we'll do it our way."

I began surveilling the house, but not on the sly. I parked a few houses down the street in a marked patrol vehicle with a barking dog in the back seat. I was all about sending a clear message. I watched cars of known dealers and drug users stop at the house. Over and over, individuals popped out of their cars and entered the house. Minutes later, the person would return to their car and drive off. It didn't take much imagination on our part to witness a traffic violation and make a stop. Most folks didn't use turn signals every time. Or they had a headlight or taillight out. Or they rolled through intersections without stopping for the stop signs.

What I couldn't figure out was why we consistently struck out on finding drugs. Every time! Mike, the guy living in the house, wasn't selling Amway products. So where were the drugs? After a few days of traffic stops with no results and continued complaints from the neighbors, I chose a more direct approach. I informed two of our department's youngest officers I was tired of the cat-and-mouse game. Tami, Chris, and I would visit the guy and explain his options. I knocked on the dude's door with the junior officers behind me. Mike opened the door and looked surprised. "I know what's going on here, Mike," I said in my best Dirty Harry voice. "You're dealing drugs, and we won't tolerate it! You have two choices: Start following the rules or leave Detroit Lakes." Mike hadn't lived in Detroit Lakes for long, and he was amassing a disproportionate number of complaints from neighbors. It was time for him to move on.

"Can we talk alone?" Mike asked as he stepped onto the landing in front of the door and shut the door behind him.

Tami and Chris repositioned to the sidewalk for a private conversation between Mike and me. "You need to talk to Patrick, the drug cop," Mike suggested.

"I don't need to talk to anybody," I responded, with the patience in my tank nearing empty.

"No, really, you need to talk to Pat," he insisted.

"Whatever!" I threw up my hands in despair. "We'll be happy to give you the extra attention you need until you stop—or we can help you pack. The choice is yours." As we left, Mike had a look on his face that led me to believe I was missing a big chunk of the whole story.

As I munched Honey-Nut Cheerios the following day, I saw my boss, Chief Kelvin B. Keena, pull into my driveway in his patrol car. *Hmmm, what does he want?* Chief Keena and I had a good relationship, but he didn't make a house call unless something was up. I invited him in, and he told me Patrick had received a call from Mike about my late-night visit. I pleaded my case, reminding my boss of the age-old battle between good and evil, emphasizing that we were the good guys. Mike's activities were corrupt and needed to be stopped.

That's when the chief divulged a well-kept secret. A few months prior, a tight group of carefully selected people, including Chief Keena and Patrick, hired Mike as an informant. The drugs were already in town, so why not create a central location where illicit transactions could take place in a controlled environment with video and audio recordings documenting activities? Mike had stepped outside with me because he didn't want our conversation recorded! Mike was *buying* drugs and documenting the purchase, not selling them.

Which is why we never found drugs in the cars we pulled over after they stopped at Mike's house.

I wasn't on the need-to-know list. Even in my fog from a short night of sleep, I saw the picture developing. "I don't agree with your tactics, Timmy," the Chief scolded. "Oops!" was the only response I could think of. In my mind, it was my job to take down a guy selling drugs in a beautiful neighborhood near an elementary school, no less. Surely, the end results of our tactics would justify the means.

Or so I thought. The us-versus-them mentality made sense to me. It was easy to adopt because people in town didn't know me as "Little Timmy from down the street." I had moved to Detroit Lakes as a police officer, so they had no other reference as they framed their opinions of me. As I became more active in the community and our three sons started school and activities, it became more challenging to discern that line between black and white, right and wrong. The idea of the "letter of the law" and the "flavor of the law" made it more emotionally taxing as I began encountering people I

went to church with

had dinner with

hung out at sporting events with

did life with.

At my core, I wasn't a robot programmed to simply identify actions that didn't fit within the parameters of laws and rules. That certainly wasn't Tim Eggebraaten, the boy, the teenager, or even the police trainee. Nevertheless, I had come to prefer making decisions solely based on an individual's behavior. Why complicate things by getting to know the person and learning what they might need to navigate life better?

I didn't notice I was losing my rhythm. I was fast becoming the person I vowed I would never be.

SIX
STRUGGLING ALONG

May 2011 kicked off "the year of the perfect storm" for our family, my team, and me, initiating events that challenged me personally, professionally, and spiritually. Denise had recently been diagnosed with stage 1A breast cancer and was undergoing chemotherapy. Our oldest son, Josh, was nearing high school graduation. And as Detroit Lakes Police Chief Keena approached retirement, I was in the running to be the next chief. By themselves, each of these life events was significant, jolting us with deep emotions and potentially disrupting our rhythm of life. All of them happening simultaneously had the potential to destroy our rhythm altogether.

But we had confidence and faith. We believed Denise's treatment at the Edith Sanford Cancer Clinic in Fargo would effectively remove all cancer in her body. The doctors, nurses, medicine, and support from family, friends, and our church were amazing. We are ecstatic to report that today, Denise is CANCER-FREE!

We were confident Josh had received an excellent education at Holy Rosary Elementary School and the Detroit Lakes Middle and High Schools. We said, "Kid, go out into the world and make a difference!" He went to college and dental school, got married, and is a dentist for the Veteran's Administration Hospital in Minneapolis. He and his wife, Mariah, made us grandparents with the births of their two adorable sons, Kit and Wes!

My training, experience, and mentorship from Chiefs Tollefson and Keena and Captains Schmidt and Goecke prepared me to apply for the department's top leadership position. I was confident I would get the job and do my best to be a good chief for the citizens of our region and the men and women of the Detroit Lakes Police Department. When I got the job and was sworn into the position in July 2011, Denise was on the road to recovery. Life was moving and grooving.

Then came Sunday, May 13, 2012, Mother's Day. Chad Jutz, among my very best friends and my police partner for 19 years, finished his patrol shift, went off-duty, and, while still in uniform, took his own life. He was 40.

As cops, we hone our ability to read people and body language and become good at it. None of us saw Chad's anguish, and his suicide completely blindsided us. With just ten months of being police chief under my belt, my head spun with the shoulda-woulda-coulda thoughts many of us experienced. Did I miss any signs Chad wasn't happy? Did I do enough for Chad? Was it something I said or did that caused him to die by suicide?

At every stage of my career—rookie, K-9 handler, patrol sergeant, investigative sergeant, and chief—I developed friendships and working relationships with my peers. I was never good, however, at asking for help. I'm the guy who requires several trips to the chiropractor because I lifted something too heavy to handle alone but was too stubborn or impatient to get assistance.

This time was different. As I surveyed the scene of my friend's death and later spoke with his grieving father, I knew this wasn't the time to be the guy who claims, "I got this." I needed guidance. My first request for help was a silent prayer to God for wisdom and clarity. The next was a call to other chiefs and command staff of agencies I had worked with throughout the years. I was pretty sure there was a group that could help in critical incidents, but I honestly couldn't remember what the team was called or how to contact them. I knew my peers would help to point me in the right direction.

A couple of days later, on May 15, I grabbed my guitar and hopped into my squad car for a 230-mile journey to the Minnesota State Capital Grounds in St. Paul. I had been asked to sing at a memorial service to honor my fallen brothers and sisters. Decades before, President John F. Kennedy signed a bill into law proclaiming May 15 as National Peace Officer Memorial Day, a yearly national remembrance of officers who gave their lives in the line of duty. It's a solemn day, with hundreds of ceremonies across the country.

Chad's death made me unsure if I could emotionally or physically fulfill my obligation, but I had to try. I recognized the immense privilege of providing music and comfort to these heroes' partners and families. The long drive to St. Paul gave me my first opportunity since Chad's death to quietly reflect. With the stereo and police radio silenced, the voices in my head hashed things out.

The task of leading my agency prevented grief from settling in. I hadn't yet had a healthy cry, and my emotions were poised to boil over like a pot of frothy potatoes on the stove.

About an hour into my trip, I spoke briefly with God. "God, help me be a positive influence on Chad's family." Chad and his wife, Shantel, were one of the first couples Denise and I met when we moved to Detroit Lakes in 1992. We became close friends, and shortly after I started with the DLPD, Chad became my partner. Both families began to grow with the births of our children, and Denise and I had the cherished honor of being asked to be godparents for the Jutz's first child and only daughter, Hailey.

Chad and I grew up together in our cop careers. We shared many moments of "you can't make this stuff up." We chased down bad guys. We helped people needing assistance. We giggled our way through pursuit driving school, unable to believe we were getting paid to push cars to their limits. Chad got motion sickness riding shotgun, so I had to let him out of the car whenever it was my turn to drive. Through tragic deaths and reprehensible crimes, we consoled each other. And we partied together, sometimes trying to mask the pain of the job.

As our careers and family dynamics changed, so did our relationship. Chad was still like a brother to me, but we hung out less socially. He was always honest with me and often challenged my decisions as sergeant or chief. His refreshing honesty was one reason I loved and respected him.

Just seconds after I uttered my prayer in my car about being there for Chad's family, my cell phone rang. I thought about ignoring it and focusing on the drive and my thoughts, but I answered. My ears were treated with the sweet sound of Hailey's voice. "Godfather!" she said. "Are you coming over tonight?"

"Not tonight, Hailey," I explained. "I'm on my way to the Twin Cities, but I'll be at your house tomorrow."

She paused briefly before she spoke again. "I don't know if I'll be able to do it, but—would you be my partner for the Father-Daughter Dance on Saturday?"

The Father-Daughter Dance was one of Chad's absolute favorite events, a number in the annual show performed by the dance school Hailey had attended for years. Chad looked forward to practicing and loved dancing with his daughter. I reminded Hailey that I was on the short list of the planet's worst dancers, but I said it would be my complete honor to be her partner.

I hung up, and now there was no holding back the tears. I pulled my cruiser to the interstate shoulder, and my previously buried emotions erupted. I didn't care what people passing me thought as they saw a parked police car with a uniformed cop sobbing inside. The episode was fierce but brief. Measured in seconds. Crying wasn't something I did. I'm unsure if it's a guy thing or my stoic Scandinavian heritage.

After my emotional outpouring, I regained my composure and continued my journey. I looked up to heaven and scolded God, saying, "God, when I said I wanted to be a positive part of Chad's family, I was thinking ten years from now, not ten seconds!" I remembered my place in my relationship with Him and thanked Him for His speedy response.

My mental fog persisted as I arrived at the Peace Officer Memorial Service. I know I sang two songs. Hundreds of people were present. I vaguely recall dozens of uniformed officers, elected officials, and dignitaries from the State of Minnesota, along with families who had lost sons and daughters in the line of duty. I remember walking off the stage between the two songs and falling to my knees. I'm pretty sure a friend came and helped me, but I can't say with certainty whether it happened or was part of a delusion induced by the trauma of Chad's death and more than 52 hours of not sleeping. I managed to pull myself together and cranked out the second song. I have no recollection of the drive home. Honestly, the rest of the day and most of the following days were a hazy dream in slow motion.

Many of us gathered at Chad and Shantel's home the following evening. A large crowd of family, cops, friends, EMS, firefighters, lawyers, and neighbors came together looking for answers and to let each other know we care. Under the dim glow of garage lights, Hailey patiently demonstrated how to execute our upcoming dance. A few father-daughter teams were there, and I know from experience that navigating an armed standoff is less stressful than learning a dance routine. The other dads seemingly had Fred

Astaire's genetics as they glided across the driveway. I moved like Frankenstein walking through quicksand. I gave us all reasons to laugh and cry.

Chad's prayer service and funeral took place on Thursday and Friday, followed by Saturday's Father-Daughter Dance. The crowd wept with sadness and joy as the father and daughter teams took the stage to perform our number. Hailey danced like a pro. Her expertise made me look—not horrible. I didn't drop her or crush her feet. Success!

In the following weeks and months, I was deep into the "what if?" game, wondering what I could have done differently or should have spotted in Chad's life. My mind churned with 20 years of witnessing tragedies that can become almost routine in law enforcement. The daily toxicity of working with pessimistic individuals wore me down to the point where I wasn't sure if any good was left in the world.

This certainly wasn't the optimism my parents had bestowed on me as I grew up.

Many times in my life, I have allowed self-doubt to seep into my conscience. "Am I qualified to lead police officers?" "Who am I to deliver a talk to emergency dispatchers?" "How many mistakes have I made and will continue to make as a father and husband?" When these thoughts permeate my consciousness, I need reminders of my positive qualities and the amazing goodness in the world.

Even in the most despairing situations, I can listen for the message of the moment. It's another technique for finding our beat and walking in the rhythm of life.

One day during the summer after Chad's death, I was lying on the couch in a deep funk, attempting to figure out which end was up, when I heard a song written by my friend Gary "Rooster"

Richter. Rooster's brother, Stan, sent me the YouTube link for "Any Moment in Time," a powerful song Rooster wrote to the melody of Bob Dylan's "Shelter from the Storm."

> *It started like any other day,*
> *and then the hammer fell.*
> *The cruelty of your fears confirmed*
> *You didn't fare so well.*
> *You started out this day with hope.*
> *It ended in such doubt.*
> *The challenges that you now face,*
> *You'll have to figure out.*

Rooster's song hit me square in my heart, reminding me of the incredible power of words and a friend's caring gesture. How could Rooster have known what I was going through? I spoke with him about his song and its impact on me. We laughed because his intended meaning wasn't anywhere close to how I absorbed it.

That's the beauty of words and music. These wake-up calls encroach on us in a way we need at that specific time. I still sing that song and can't imagine any other interpretation each time those lyrics emerge from my mouth. Yet I also know that someone listening may receive a different message, precisely what they need to hear at that precise *moment in time!*

I heard the necessary message at precisely the right instant.

These messages bombard us constantly. We need to be willing to actively listen and decipher them immediately. I promise messages always come our way if we are ready to hear and act.

The Jutz family and me

SEVEN
STAND BY ME

With the help of many people, we managed to get through the next few months as a team and as a family. We had more challenges that summer within the department, and I again leaned on my support network. My first year as chief was such a doozy that Moorhead, Minnesota, Police Chief Dave Ebinger, an experienced leader reared in Arkansas, asked me in his Southern twang, "Chief, what powers did you piss off for all this to happen?"

The support I received was incredible. I had been in the criminal justice business for 23 years—more than two decades of the good, bad, and ugly. I had seen people at their ultimate best and witnessed true heroes make a real difference. I had also seen people do horrible, unspeakable things to senior citizens, children, family members, strangers, and themselves. For most of those years, however, I had neglected one giant piece of the puzzle: myself.

My concern had rightfully been
How am I going to be a leader for my team?
How can I be there for my own family?

What about Chad's family? How can I be a positive role model for his kids?

It would be amazing if there were a chapter in the *Police Chief Manual* on how to properly handle a situation like this: How to be a leader for my team, a friend to my partner's family, a good husband to my wife, an attentive father to my three sons, and a solid steward of myself mentally, physically, and spiritually. Unfortunately, I wasn't aware of such a book, and I didn't have a checklist in my Policy and Procedure Manual to guide me through this.

Mental health professionals point to a phenomenon called "cumulative stress," a buildup that impacts a person's bodily functioning, cognitive output, mood, and ability to function healthily. I suppose Chad's death was another straw on the proverbial camel's back, and amassed junk from other traumas surfaced in my mind. I had difficulty sleeping. When I was awake, I couldn't focus. Images of past incidents played over and over in my brain.

I didn't pay much attention to what I was experiencing until we hosted a regional Chief of Police meeting in Detroit Lakes the autumn after Chad's death. At the social gathering the night before the meeting, the chaplain of our association, Pastor Dan Carlson, a retired chief himself, approached me and said, "How are you doing, Tim?" I said, "I'm great, Dan! How are you?" He said again, "How are you doing, Tim?" I reiterated, "I'm GREAT, Dan. How are you?" As if he hadn't heard me the first two times, he asked me again, "How are you doing, Tim?" I had to ask him where he was going with this line of questioning.

Pastor Dan reminded me that the past year had taken me through some challenging events. He suggested I may still be in "chief mode" by taking care of others, and perhaps I should consider having a professional examine *my* overall mental health. He gave me the phone number of Steve Wickelgren, a Minneapolis Police Department Sergeant who was also a trained therapist and psychologist. "Nobody will find out," Dan suggested. "You can pay Steve in cash. It will all be confidential."

I couldn't help but wonder if Pastor Dan had mystical powers and was somehow inside my head, watching the two decades of colorful images and mental videos I was reliving. It wasn't until several years later that I found out a friend and peer, Moorhead Police Deputy Chief Shannon Monroe, had asked Dan that night to check on me because he recognized my rhythm seemed off. It isn't a stretch to believe this string of events likely changed and saved my life.

The stigma and myths surrounding mental health are real, and I certainly wasn't immune to having reservations about seeing a "shrink." I thought the whole world would somehow know. They would think I was crazy and talk about me behind my back. I resisted calling anybody for a month or so, and I finally called "Doctor Jeff," a local psychologist I had known and trusted for several years.

When I made the appointment to see Dr. Jeff, I felt like a junior high boy trying to call the cute girl he liked in school. Several times, I dialed a few digits and hung up before mustering the courage to punch in the complete number and make the appointment. I consciously chose Dr. Jeff, who practiced at Sanford Clinic in Detroit Lakes, instead of going somewhere I wouldn't be known. I felt this was a big first step to ensuring I was okay. Going to Minneapolis or somewhere else might have been more discreet and easier, but easier isn't necessarily better.

As I walked up to the receptionist desk at the clinic on that sunny October day, I had the perception that everybody would assume I was in the middle of a mental breakdown. It didn't help that I was in full uniform—white uniform shirt, polyester pants, full duty belt, and shiny badge—and I had been in the community for over 20 years as a police officer and entertainer. People knew me, and for some reason, that made it even more critical for me to own this journey.

I checked in and went to the waiting room on the left. Again, I had a misguided belief that people with a boo-boo on their knee went to the waiting room to the right, and crazy people went to the left. I was sure that every eye was on me, and they questioned whether someone in that condition should carry a firearm!

As I completed the paperwork, I grumbled to myself and wished Dr. Jeff had opened the back door of the clinic to let me enter discretely. I would later recognize this as part of the healing process. Shortcuts may feel better in the short haul, but taking care of challenges the right way helps make a more positive and long-lasting outcome.

Dr. Jeff and I had a great conversation. In addition to talking about Post Traumatic GROWTH, we discussed the signs and symptoms of Post Traumatic Stress Disorder (PTSD) and cumulative stress. He explained to me how the brain processes events and that the brain can get overloaded by a traumatic experience. It takes a while for our minds to break it down and deal with it. "It's like a funnel," he said. "Our life events get put into the funnel-shaped hopper. Ideally, our processed thoughts and feelings come out the tube at the bottom as healthy and well-adjusted thoughts."

The world's weight lifted from my shoulders as I learned what I was going through was normal, and I wasn't alone. I needed to monitor my progress and access other forms of treatment if these dark feelings lingered too long. Dr. Jeff taught me that one effective way to deal with the images I was reliving wasn't to repress them. "Let the video in your mind play through instead of trying to shut it off," Dr. Jeff suggested.

Another action point the Doc shared with me was to talk to others about my experiences. Initially, I was hesitant, but I slowly began communicating these experiences with others, which was fulfilling.

I quickly discovered that listeners found benefit in hearing my story. They might have already been thinking about similar experiences, and it helped them hear examples from another perspective. The double-whammy effect of helping me process my traumatic experiences AND helping someone else was fantastic.

I don't believe anything happens by accident or happenstance. Each of us is alive for a purpose. Everyone we meet in our journey through life is put in our path for a reason. We may never fully understand that purpose, and, likely, we'll never even know what impact we have on others. It's imperative, though, to treat our relationships with strangers, friends, co-workers, and family members with the realization of the preciousness of these bonds.

We have all failed miserably at this many times, and there's a chance we will again drop the ball. Carefully considering our relationship with others in our relatively short time on earth will hopefully cause us to stand by others, a dynamic best summed up by powerful lyrics in the 1960s song by Ben E. King, Mike Stoller, and Jerry Leiber, "Stand by Me."

Recorded more than 400 times by various artists, including me, this song remains as relevant as ever. What do those lyrics mean to you? Is the person in the song asking a friend to stick close to them? Are they praying and asking God to stand by them through their troubling times? Maybe it's a spouse who stays with their partner and loves them unconditionally despite the partner's poor choices, habits, and addictions.

The meaning of "Stand by Me" became distinctly clear in those tough years of 2011 and 2012. I needed God, peers, family, and friends to stand by me. Always. I can't go it alone. Ever. We weren't designed to go through this gig of life solo.

I have a tangible reminder of these all-important connections I carry in my pocket. It's with me no matter where I go or what I encounter.

Challenge coins, metal medallions one to two inches or so in diameter, have been associated with the military for many years. Their origin is debated, but they can signify membership in an organization and remind the holder of belonging to a unit. One story suggests the coins originated during World War One when a United States Air Force lieutenant designed coins for his unit members. The legend says the Germans captured the Lieutenant. They took all his belongings except for the coin he carried in a pouch tied around his neck. When the lieutenant managed to escape, he was confronted by Allied troops, who thought he might be an enemy until he produced the coin. It bore his unit's markings, and the Allies determined he stood on their side.

Regardless of their origin, the coins became popular in the 1960s during the Vietnam War. Coins vary in size and color. They can cost $5 to $25 each, and enthusiasts collect and trade them.

During much of my career in law enforcement, I was a member of the Northwest Minnesota Fraternal Order of Police (FOP) Lodge #8. While many FOP Chapters across the country serve as a labor union for rank-and-file officers, in Northwest Minnesota, we stressed the organization's fraternal piece and avoided ranks. Within the FOP, a police chief or sheriff was equal to a line officer. We got together for beers, raised money for kids and cops in need, and shared the brotherhood and sisterhood of being a cop. When a cop needed something in an emergency, we were there for the brother or sister, offering help or sending a card to let them know they were on our minds during a difficult time.

Our lodge designed Lodge 8 challenge coins and sold them as a lodge fundraiser. The coins were beautiful. On the front was our lodge's "slanted 8," like the number of famed NASCAR driver

Dale Earnhardt, Jr. The back depicted St. Michael, the patron saint of those in law enforcement and the military. The coin quickly became my favorite, and I carried it constantly in my right front pocket. It reminded me I belong to a large organization of brothers and sisters. Although we bicker like family now and then, we are there for each other. The coin helped me focus on why I got into law enforcement in the first place and on the bond that exists. I have three biological sisters—all older than me—but I never had a biological brother, so this organization gave me many brothers and sisters.

The coins were sold and traded as time passed, and getting one of the original Lodge 8 coins was becoming increasingly difficult. One night, I was having a few beers with friends at a friend's house, and Chad Jutz was there. My partner, "Jutzy," had become one of my best friends, and as cops working the night shift, we had faced down some crazy stuff together. Chad wasn't a member of the FOP but was the poster child for what the brotherhood was all about, so I gave Chad my Lodge 8 challenge coin, telling him that he was "more FOP than most FOP guys I knew," and I wanted him to have my coin. At first, Chad resisted, but he finally accepted the gift.

A couple of weeks later, Chad returned my coin and said he wanted to earn it because he knew how much it meant to me. I reluctantly took it back and eventually gave it to my nephew, who was serving in the US Army. I got lucky and got a replacement from a brother within our lodge. The world was right again!

After Chad died in 2012, I had the honor of singing a couple of songs at his prayer service and funeral. As he lay in his casket wearing his purple dress shirt, I reached into my right pants pocket, pulled out my Lodge 8 coin, and tucked it into his shirt pocket. I leaned close and whispered, "Go ahead and try to give it back to me now, buddy"!

I was again without my Lodge 8 challenge coin and struggling to find one. One afternoon, an off-duty FOP brother, Ruben, came to my office with one of his teenage sons by his side. My brother shook my hand and placed a Lodge 8 coin into my hand. Ruben had heard what I had done with my coin and wanted me to have his. I hoped his teenage son could someday grasp what that moment meant to his father and me. The coin is just a chunk of metal with no real monetary value, but to my brother and me, that coin was much more. It symbolizes everything right in the world and within our brotherhood, a concrete sign that we stand with each other without fail.

That specific coin remained in my right front pocket for a couple of years until it shook loose while I was flying around in a four-wheeler in the Mexican Baja dunes outside Cabo San Lucas, Mexico. While losing the coin was disappointing, the trip was excellent. I replaced the coin with another, and I still carry it everywhere I go to remind me of the men and women who proudly serve in our law enforcement agencies and armed services. Every moment of every day, I feel that challenge coin in my pocket.

The coin I designed

A few years ago, I designed a coin of my own. I wanted a way to keep my mom's legacy of "I Am, I Can, I WILL" alive, so I inscribed the motto onto a coin along with the words, "Find Your Beat, the Rhythm of Life." On the other side of the coin, it simply says "CHALLENGE." The coin is a physical reminder that it can be very challenging at times to remember we can control our attitude and reaction to situations. Most events in our lives lie outside our control, but we always have a choice in our attitude!

I challenge you to choose a physical reminder to remind yourself that *you* control your attitude, and *you* can stand with others in their time of need—and that they will faithfully stand with you.

EIGHT
AWAKENING

When I was 48 years old, I decided on a plan to retire from law enforcement at 50. In Minnesota, we could begin to draw on our Public Employee Retirement Association (PERA) Police Retirement Fund when we reach 50. The optimum age was 55, with a financial penalty assessed on disbursements for each year before that magical age. I have never been very good at math and remembering numbers. Denise is the financial guru in our family, and I rely heavily on her expertise and wisdom. I just knew I probably wouldn't live to 55 if I stuck around as the police chief.

Don't get me wrong. The staff at the Detroit Lakes Police Department was excellent. I was blessed to work with true heroes —men and women who consistently went above and beyond the call of duty. Moreover, the citizens of Detroit Lakes appreciated our service. Their representatives, our city council, were women and men who supported the DLPD and struck a delicate balance of support and well-intentioned questions. Our budget was fair for citizens and the city, ensuring officers were well-equipped and adequately trained. Pound for pound, I would stack our team against any in the country.

Despite those significant reasons to feel great about my work, the job weighed on me. The cumulative stress of serving as an officer and then chief beat on me like the waves of Lake Superior constantly pounding the shoreline, wearing it down. For years, I had coached others, "If you're not happy with your path, change it!" It was time to examine my life and apply that same wisdom to my own choices.

At one particularly relevant Minnesota Chiefs of Police Association conference, I listened to a panel of retired chiefs discuss their decisions to shift gears. Retired Eden Prairie Police Chief Dan Carlson (Pastor Dan) shared his story of choosing to retire at 49½ years, six months before being eligible to draw even a dime of his pension. Hearing Dan recount how he recognized his occupation had become unhealthy for him and how he included his wife and family in the discussion was pivotal for me. I knew I could hang on a couple more years, but why push to hit 55?

When I announced I would step away from the cop world at the ripe old age of 50, there was scrutiny from some.

"Why is he quitting?"

"Was he fired?"

"I guess he couldn't handle it!"

Many expressed their appreciation for my nearly 25 years with the DLPD. More than once, I heard, "It must be nice to retire so young. I should have been a cop!" I wished I could have plugged a USB drive into their brain and instantly uploaded all my thoughts and experiences. Maybe then they would understand. The best I could do was mumble under my breath. *Whatever!*

Retiring was more than a date on the calendar. It would be a long process of rewiring an internal alarm system on high alert my entire adult life. I didn't want to lose who I was as an officer, but I needed to redirect that energy.

As a cop, it was essential I make quick assumptions about people based on their body language, appearance, clothing, location, time of day, and so on. I was often focused on what could happen if they had a weapon. Or I asked myself, "What did that person do wrong—or what are they about to do?" It was all necessary for survival, and it bothered me when other officers were lax in paying attention to officer safety concerns.

The daily difficulty, however, was shutting down when I was off duty. I continued scanning for people or a feeling that something was out of place. As I entered a restaurant, church, or other public space, I constantly looked for escape routes and always sat with my back away from the door so I could surveil the entire room. I perceived most people as potential threats rather than potential friends. When I asked someone, "How do I know you?" it meant their face looked familiar, but I was trying to place them. Had we met at a bar? The gym? Were they a crime victim? Or someone I arrested? If our encounter had been adversarial, it would have been awkward for both of us.

A few months before I retired, I organized my final retreat for the police chiefs in Region 4 of the Minnesota Chiefs of Police Association (MCPA). Our retreats allowed law enforcement leaders to gather, network, and learn from one another. Throughout my career, participation in associations like the MCPA was crucial to my personal and professional growth. The relationships I nurtured helped me through the darkest times in my career. As a young patrol officer, I found my crew at Drug Abuse Resistance Education (DARE) training and conferences. For seven years, the United States Police Canine Association (USPCA) connected me with some of the bravest men and women I've ever met and their larger-than-life K-9 partners. When I rose into department leadership, I needed additional groups. I was no longer one of the guys. My perspective broadened to making the best decisions for my team and the citizens we served. I discovered that leadership can be lonely. Actively participating in groups like the MCPA allowed me to access leaders from agencies large and small, chiefs and command staff with a wide range of experiences. I leaned heavily on that camaraderie.

As I prepared for this final retreat, I invited Steve Wickelgren, the Minneapolis Police Department sergeant who was also a licensed therapist and counselor. He had recently retired from law enforcement. "Wellness" was still a buzzword, but law enforcement leaders were beginning to walk the talk and bring in professionals to help frontline officers and staff. "Suck it up, Buttercup" had been the mindset for generations, and it was exciting to see that mentality challenged. My personal experience with trauma and therapy made Steve our obvious choice.

As Steve addressed our group of a couple dozen police chiefs, he discussed an exercise he had often used with clients experiencing stress. "If you're comfortable playing along," he said, "close your eyes and take a deep breath."

Are you freaking kidding me? I thought. This room was full of seasoned cops who had risen to the role of agency leader. We had each been through a lot. We were tough. We weren't going to close our eyes for a dip into this hippie-voodoo crap. Well, as far as I could tell, we did because my eyes were closed.

Steve's voice wasn't as low as Barry White's but was equally as smooth, and he took our minds on a journey. Steve had us imagine sitting by a lush forest stream. His descriptions of the trees and sky made it easy to see the setting. As he helped us see a stream, he suggested we follow a leaf floating on the ripples. I could visualize the leaf slowly drifting down the stream. He described how the leaf would then go out of sight.

On the next pass of the leaf, Steve suggested we put something on it. "How about a purple elephant?" Steve prompted. Sure enough, the giant purple elephant rode a leaf down the river, and it even smiled at me as it passed by. As the elephant disappeared from my field of view, Steve suggested we put something else on the leaf—a word or an image of something we were thinking about. I put our department's new record management system on the leaf on the next pass. I guess it was on my mind! Steve said the goal wasn't to suppress the thought or image but to observe it as it went by and let it slip out of sight. We were instructed to watch it again if it returned as it navigated the winding river.

A few months after that retreat, I was enjoying retirement. I called Steve and asked what that exercise was called. I told him it profoundly affected me and the stress levels I was feeling. He called it "mindfulness." I'm an educated person with a plethora of life experience, but I don't think I had heard that term before then. If I had, I forgot it, or my mind wasn't ready to process it. Either way, I wanted more!

However, as I continued adjusting to retirement, life intervened. Toward the end of 2016, my mom lay dying of cancer, and I soon discovered I badly needed to deal with a personal issue I had ignored most of my life.

Mom received hospice care at home, where a hospital bed took over my parents' living room. Dad, my sisters, and I took turns caring for her as she neared the end. I felt like the Little Drummer Boy, unsure of what gift I could bring Mom, but I knew she loved music. She had always supported me like the excellent mother she was, even when the sounds I blatted from my trumpet in my beginner days could make anyone's ears bleed. As I sat on the couch near her bed, picking my guitar while my sister Kristen gently caressed mom's hair, I was singing "How Great Thou Art" when Kristen quietly said, "She's gone. Keep singing." I don't pretend to know how much my mom heard or understood during the last few weeks of her life, but I trust she could hear me singing and that it comforted her. It certainly gave me solace to have the opportunity to play for her.

Amid our grieving and helping my dad adjust to his new life alone, a problem of my own making finally caught up with me, leaving me no chance to escape.

NINE
ONE FOR THE ROAD

Is it possible to trace many years of poor decisions back to the source? I may have come close. Throughout most of my life, I wrestled with finding reasonable limits related to alcohol consumption. I yearned to be like Tom Selleck's character in the hit TV show "Blue Bloods." New York Police Department Commissioner Frank Reagan could savor one small glass of scotch after a hard day at the office. Our society is fascinated with alcohol, and it seemed to me like liquor and good times were joined at the liver. I had difficulty limiting myself to just one beer or to one glass of anything with booze in it. What began as having to fight through the disgusting jolt and acquire a taste for spirits became a torrid love affair with the liquid. It's not hard to backtrack my steps from a 51-year-old newly retired police chief to my 12-year-old self, scratching for a way to fit in.

Ahh! Beautiful summertime in northwest Minnesota! The mosquitoes were gathering and plotting their season of blood-sucking and mayhem, the sky was Robin-egg blue, and the leaves on the trees peeked out of their buds from their frozen slumber. It was May 1979, and sixth grade was now behind us. My friends and I had the next few months to relax and prepare for junior high.

Even though our small school building housed everyone from kindergarten to 12th grade, junior high was still a big-dang-deal. The excitement built as a few 12-year-old friends met in the woods for our no-girls-allowed camping trip. A clearing among the trees near the Red Lake River provided a perfect spot for our tents and security from our parents, the Polk County sheriff's deputies, and Freddy Krueger himself.

The woods were only a half-mile from our town, and it was a utopia for us with trails to ride bicycles or motorcycles, plenty of wildlife like deer and squirrels, and trees providing cover as we shot at each other with BB guns.

A .177 caliber BB leaves a mark! If any of us were lucky enough to own a pump BB gun, we would mandate a one-pump rule that was seldom followed. "Hey, Jay! Is that a Crossman Pump BB Gun? Cool! Remember, you can't pump that sucker more than once!" Yet I could hear him pump that stock—way past once. The scar on my left index finger and the dent in my Daisy Red Ryder prove that a projectile will break the skin if your "enemy" defies the rule and primes his gun ten times. Although, at times, we wore long johns to protect our legs, butts, and privates, we never thought to include any eye protection.

We set up camp near a spot we called "The Devil's Hole," a small but seemingly bottomless pond at the bottom of a large crater. As a young man, I spent many hours there, communing with the abundant nature.

As our fire crackled, we shared our dreams of girls and the future when someone said, "You guys want some of this?" I don't remember who brought it, but a bottle of Cherry Sloe Gin made its way around the group. I had sipped my dad's brandy on a fishing trip once, which tasted like I imagined jet fuel would. The Sloe

Gin was different. It was sweet as candy but went down like cough medicine.

"My teeth feel funny!" "Do your lips feel numb?" I don't know if the other guys had any experience with booze, but this was new for me. As we continued passing the bottle, my dizziness was unlike anything I had ever felt. I loved it! It was euphoric until one of the guys puked up the slimy red mixture. Trying to sleep with the tent spinning like the tilt-a-whirl wasn't a treat. Still, the upsides of the experience outdid the downsides, and I was now one of the guys.

The next day, my family and I were heading out on a camping trip of our own. While cruising down the road in the maroon 1976 Impala with the windows down, my sister Stacey blurted, "Timmy's been drinking!"

How did she know? More importantly, why was she ratting me out?

Mom replied, "Timmy knows better than that."

I was off the hook. Consequence-free drinking was easier than I thought it would be. What could go wrong?

As I entered junior high, sports gave me ample reason to abstain from alcohol. Opportunities for extra-curricular sports for boys in Fisher were limited to football, basketball, and track. Football and track were high on my list of favorites. I was sure my 160-pound frame at the right guard position on the offensive line wouldn't put me on the radar for the Minnesota Vikings. Yet football was life, and I didn't want to mess it up by getting busted with alcohol.

In my sophomore year of high school, I attended a girls' basketball game in the neighboring town of Crookston. My friend Scott was dating a Crookston girl, and he told me she had a friend who wanted to meet me. As we walked into the CHS gymnasium, the school fight song played to the tune of "The Minnesota

Rouser," I stuck my shoulders a bit farther back to ensure the big "F" on my Fisher Flyer letterman's jacket protruded. The letter even had a couple of pins stuck to it, showing the world my accomplishments and garnering the attention of the Crookston Pirates. Crookston and Fisher are only eight miles apart, and while we weren't huge rivals in sports, some frowned on Fisher kids dating Crookston kids.

"There they are!" Scott directed my attention to the bleachers on our left. Nine rows up, near the steps, was Tammy, Scott's girlfriend. To Tammy's right was the love of my life. "There's no such thing as 'Love at first sight,'" I've heard many times. That may be true for some people, but I was smitten when I saw green eyes as I had never seen before. Denise was shy, and we exchanged awkward hellos. She was 14, and her fifteenth birthday was only a month away.

Scott and I took Denise to Godfather's Pizza a few weeks later. That might not sound like a date, but it sure felt like a date as Scott faded from my sight and Denise hijacked my attention. This outing would be a point of controversy for years to come. When I tell people, "Denise and I started dating when she was 14!" it sounds a little creepy. But she held my hand as we rode in the back seat of Scott's mom's Ford Thunderbird. It was awesome having our private chauffeur.

Denise wasn't much of a heavy partier as our courtship continued, but she tolerated me whooping it up when I wasn't in sports. We attended a few summer parties together, and my alcohol consumption began to ramp up. I remember driving away from one party and needing to pull over to puke. My friend Mike pulled up behind me and walked up to see if I was okay, only to find himself standing in what appeared to be a pile of liquified rice. I wiped my chin and continued driving to get Denise home. Being unsafe to drive and putting others in danger never crossed my mind. I was having fun, and that was all there was to it.

Denise had one more year of high school left when I went off to Moorhead State University. I had broken both my ankles in a motorcycle accident that summer. When I attended freshman orientation, I still had two casts on my feet, giving me a built-in conversation starter with strangers.

It was my first time away from home, and the drinking seed had firmly taken root. The gloves came off, and I punched the party scene square in the chops. I knew only one other person at the college when I started, so I had 7,000 potential friends to meet, and I could reinvent myself. I had been able to illegally purchase alcohol at a couple of liquor stores around home since I was 16, so I was disappointed when the establishments surrounding three universities made me wait a few months until I was legal at 19.

Alcohol was still easy to obtain. I limited my partying to only the days that ended in Y, and I was having the time of my life. The whole classroom thing was a drag, so I opted to pass on many of them. I attended a going-away gathering for a friend during a trip home that first year. After a night of partying, I loaded up the 1972 VW Super Beetle with a couple of friends and headed home. I buzzed through an intersection without stopping for a flashing red traffic light as we were leaving North Dakota, and a Grand Forks police officer pulled me over just as we crossed the bridge into Minnesota.

You would think that getting pulled over by a Grand Forks, North Dakota, Police Officer in East Grand Forks, Minnesota, would have scared me enough to get me to get off the road. The officer warned me, and she let us go. Instead of calling it a night and heading for home, the warning boosted my confidence, and I decided to go *back* to Grand Forks to get fuel.

As I pulled up to the gas pump, a different Grand Forks Police Officer swept in behind me. He got out and approached me as I pumped my gas. "How's it going tonight?" he questioned.

"It's going great, officer! How is your night?"

"Do you have your driver's license on you?"

Handing him my debit card was probably a clue I was pickled.

"Let's do some tests, shall we?"

Walking nine steps didn't seem to be a problem for me, even in my cowboy boots. The alphabet? Easy breezy! This wouldn't take too long. I know I had felt far more intoxicated during prior driving incidents, so I felt confident I would ace his tests. He would undoubtedly apologize and let me go home.

"You're under arrest for suspected DWI," he said, putting me in the back of the squad car without handcuffing me. My cousin was a Grand Forks police officer, so I assumed this guy was being nice by not cuffing me. The pit in my stomach grew with each block we drove closer to the jail. As we walked in, panic swept over me. "This is really happening!" I said to myself as the jail staff emptied my pockets.

I don't remember much about the booking process. At some point, I submitted to a blood test and then was put in a cell with a guy named Charlie. Somehow, everyone knew Charlie's name, as if he were a regular resident of the Crowbar Hotel. He mumbled something to me, but he was slurring worse than me. They offered me a phone call, but I declined. I wanted to ride this one out on my own. I never once thought of my parents waiting for me to get home and wondering what happened to me. They didn't know until they called my friend Brad's mom and dad in the morning, and Brad told them I had been arrested.

When my dad came to pick me up the following day, my exaggerated confidence was still in high gear, leading me to believe that the blood test would come back under .10 and that I would beat this charge. "Don't say anything," I instructed my father. When he asked me where my car was, I realized that the alcohol created gaps in my memory. After driving around for a while, we found the Super Beetle, and I drove home.

The blood test results were mailed to me a few weeks later, and they weren't under .10. They weighed in at a whopping .17. A big, fat FLUNK! How could I fight that in court? The traffic stop was legitimate; I was driving, and I was the one who completely lost count of how many beers I had slammed.

My parents and coaches instilled ownership of our actions in me. So, I went to court and told the judge I was guilty. He sentenced me to probation and gave me credit for the night in the slammer. Because we were in North Dakota when I got stopped and had a Minnesota driver's license, there were technical issues between the states I felt didn't concern me. "The states will figure out what to do with my license," I surmised. I lost my driving privileges in North Dakota, but my Minnesota driver's license was still valid in Minnesota and every other state except North Dakota. A few years later, I was reminded of this detail when I interned with the Fargo, North Dakota, Police Department. I drove to the Fargo PD every day of the ten-week internship, and it wasn't until I applied for a job with the department that a lieutenant discovered my suspended driving privileges.

"Oops!" I said.

"You're going to have to get reinstated if you want to work for us," he explained.

One of the reinstatement requirements was to attend a DWI seminar with other DWI offenders. I was entering my senior year of college, and being excluded from driving in North Dakota rankled me. I was amazed to find I was the only one in class who was guilty. Everyone else in the class told me the cops or an ex-girlfriend had set them up. Or they were victims of a faulty alcohol test.

When it was my turn to explain my presence, I said, "Well, I went to a going-away party for a friend, drank a ton of beer, drove my '72 VW Super Beetle, got pulled over once, was somehow released, and got pulled over a second time while I was getting fuel. I was drunk, got caught, and went to jail." My fellow offenders looked at me as if I had violated some unspoken pact by taking responsibility for my actions.

The next requirement was an Alcohol Problem Assessment or APA. I don't remember much about the one-on-one interview, but whatever BS I fed the interviewer, he bought it, shook my hand at the end, and said, "I wish I had a son like you!" What? This was the validation I needed to prove I didn't have a drinking problem. The issue wasn't the cocktails or driving while impaired. It was getting *caught* and arrested.

When I charged into my career as a police officer with the Detroit Lakes Police Department, I was the stereotypical new cop. The laws of our society were black and white—no gray. "How fast can I go before I get a ticket?" people often asked. "Well, if the speed limit is 55, then at 56, you technically could get a ticket." That was my typical response. The badge I was issued and the oath I swore had the power to deprive another human being of their freedom, and I took that authority seriously. It was my duty to enforce the law without exception.

The easiest way to carry out my duties was to do it the same way across the board, treating everyone equally. Some department old-timers enjoyed this because they could sic me on a city council member with expired license plate tabs, and I would write that person a ticket, not knowing or caring about repercussions. I'm sure others in the department were wondering if the new kid's attitude was the wave of the future. It likely felt radical for some, and they probably wanted to get rid of me.

With that mindset locked in, I didn't need to apply emotions. I would hold the offender accountable if an act were against the law. It's embarrassing to think back on what a hard-ass I was, but it was a significant piece of my personal and professional growth.

TEN
DONE WITH MY DEMON

During the early years of my patrol career, drunk drivers were high on my list of offenders I wanted to get off the streets. It wasn't uncommon for me to notch more than one DWI arrest during an eight-hour shift, and I took satisfaction in knowing the arrestee wouldn't be able to hurt anyone or themselves that evening. I don't have many regrets for making those arrests or the citations I issued during my career, but it's not lost on me that I was guilty of many of the same infractions. The hypocrisy of it all disheartens me.

My aggressiveness as a patrol officer garnered me favor from some of my peers and disapproval from others. I quickly developed a reputation as a brash and cocky young cop who didn't take crap from anyone. My hot button was any 16-to-19-year-old white male who challenged my authority.

The complaints to my bosses were starting to pile up, although only one was sustained, and the rest were classified as exonerated or not sustained. Chief Tollefson and Captain Schmidt were "old school" and didn't bring many complaints to my attention. I asked Captain Schmidt about it once, and he said, "If I didn't get any complaints about you, I wouldn't think you were doing your job." I believe they felt it was part of the deal to have an officer aggressively enforce the law. It wasn't until Chief Keena told me during one of his verbal reprimand sessions with me, "Timmy, where there's smoke, there's fire."

Did he call me "Timmy? My mom and grandma are the only people who can call me that!

"I'm not sure what you mean, boss," I replied. "I'm just out there doing my job." How the chief refrained from reaching across his desk and wrapping his huge mitts around my neck during his coaching sessions is beyond me.

"Well, Timmy, look at Gary. Gary makes as many arrests as you do, but I never get complaints about him harassing people or calling someone a 'maggot.' How does Gary do it?"

I'm thankful for the leaders I worked for as a police officer. Chief Tollefson, Chief Keena, Captain Paul Goecke, and Captain Ed Schmidt got gray hairs dealing with me, but these leaders all kept up their encouragement and mentoring.

Chief Tollefson had hired me, and I had heard stories about him and Captain Schmidt and their lives "back in the day." Both men openly talked about their challenges with alcohol early on and how they got a handle on it before it could ruin their careers. Their words were seeds planted in the fertile ground of my brain but would lay dormant for several years.

As my career continued, I went to school for three months to get a police K-9 partner, Quincy. I was promoted to sergeant, taught Drug Abuse Resistance Education (DARE), attended another three-month leadership school, worked in investigations, and became police chief. Each phase of the career brought exciting challenges, rewards, and stressors. Along with my career growth came the surge of my drinking problems.

Many conferences I attended included an open bar at hospitality events. I hit the partying hard and tried to maintain the façade of keeping it all together. Later in life, while writing this book, I realized I'm far more introverted than I had ever recognized, and I'm insecure in many social settings. I used alcohol to level the playing field and compensate for that insecurity. With a drink in my hand, my confidence grew, and I could talk about anything with anybody. Toss a guitar into my hands, and my insecurity vanished completely.

I made it through my career without my drinking causing major public embarrassment. For over five and a half years as chief, I was blessed with an amazing staff, and working with these professional men and women was a fantastic career highlight. On the night of my retirement gathering and 50th birthday celebration, I partied until 3:00 AM with family and friends. It made me wonder if I could attend future events without taking on a rockstar persona and partying like I was 20. I also began worrying about getting wasted at future family events.

Within a year after retirement, I entertained in the beer garden at a semi-professional baseball game across the Red River in Fargo. This gig was always one of my favorites because the game started at 12:30 in the afternoon, and I started playing immediately following the game, which meant I would be done around 5:00 PM and home at a reasonable hour. The best part was the fun-loving crowd and free beer! Not only did I get paid for the gig, but all I had to do was signal the bartenders my glass was empty, and voila, the glass was full of cold golden goodness. I used to keep track of how many glasses I emptied, but that afternoon's audience was epic, and counting beers wasn't on my mind. With the sun beating down on us, my speakers blaring, and the crowd loving my cover songs and singing along, I wasn't holding back.

My son Luke was at the game and the beer garden, and he helped me pack my gear after the gig. I was in full party mode and didn't want the night to end. He said he was meeting some friends at a fun Fargo bar. "I'll give you a ride, my boy!" I told him. "Hop in!" We joined his friends, and we were greeted with a tray of plastic glasses of beer. I felt like a college kid again, hanging out with my friends. Reality check! I was a 50-year-old retired cop hanging out with his 22-year-old son and HIS friends.

My beer counter still was non-functioning when I figured it was time to hit the road. As I fired up the Subaru and locked in HOME on the GPS, a Safe-and-Sober Public Service Announcement came on the radio: "If you drink, designate. This message is brought to you by Anheuser-Busch." I remember verbally saying to myself, "Yeah, right." The fact that I had to use the GPS should have been the first clue I had no right to be behind the wheel. I certainly knew my way home. Luke asked me if I would be okay, and I told him I would be—a rotten position for a father to put his son in.

As I returned to Minnesota and zipped through Moorhead, I was plugging my phone into the charger when I saw emergency lights behind me. *CRAP!* I pulled into a parking lot, and the police car continued following me. Half of me hoped the officer was someone I knew, and the other half hoped for a stranger. I was having drunken flashbacks to my first DWI 31 years before.

The Moorhead police officer, Mike, was a guy I had never met. He had a K-9 partner, and Mike reminded me of myself at his age. I asked him what sergeant was on duty. The sergeant was an old friend, but thankfully, he was unavailable. "Never mind," I said. I'm so glad I didn't drag him into my mess.

I knew I was drunk even before I bombed the field sobriety tests. "You're under arrest for suspicion of drunk driving." How many times had I uttered that phrase during my career? Somehow, I knew those were precisely the words I needed to hear. I was hoping for some form of professional courtesy, but I knew this was the right thing for the officer to do. I screwed up, and I was going to jail.

As we walked into the Clay County Jail, where I had begun my career nearly three decades before, I saw Nancy, one of the correctional officers I started with. I don't know who was more disappointed, Nancy or me, but I think I felt worse. She gave me a glance that said, "It'll be okay." I know she had given that look to so many others.

I used up all my lawyer-searching time, not even trying to call an attorney. What would an attorney tell me? "You're drunk! Take the breath test!" I consented to a breath test and scored another big, fat flunk!

"The good news," said the arresting officer, "is that you're under the gross misdemeanor limit, so I won't be impounding your license plates, and you can be released to a sober party."

Who the hell am I going to call?

I called Denise to let her know where I was at. After all these years of her putting up with my partying, I thought this would end our marriage—and who would blame her? Not me!

"Hi there," I slurred.

"Where are you?" Her voice told me her intuition was already at work, and she knew exactly where I was. It was a scenario I'm sure she had played out in her mind night after lonely night as I was out doing gigs. I didn't expect her to come to get me, and I didn't want her driving the 45 miles while she was upset.

I made several other calls to friends in the area but didn't get through for a while. The jail staff had me change into orange jail clothes, booked me, and put me in a holding cell. A short time later, Brad, a good friend, came to pick me up. It was reminiscent of my dad coming to pick up my drunk butt from jail. "Get some sleep, Tim. It'll be okay," he said as he showed me to the guest room in his house.

How will it EVER be okay? I've been arrested for my second DWI in 31 years. CANADA will NEVER let me into their country; DENISE is going to DUMP me, and the MEDIA is going to fly with the story of the FORMER CHIEF getting ARRESTED for driving DRUNK. They'll plaster my MUGSHOT on the news, and my DAD and my KIDS will all be so DISAPPOINTED.

My friend and I were silent the following morning as he drove me back to my car. I almost expected to see the 1972 VW Super Beetle waiting for me. Instead, the Subaru Outback was there. I swear, even the car was disappointed in me. The headlights avoided eye contact, and the wagon transported me home with first-class silent treatment.

When I got home to Denise, she had been crying all night, and the "I'm sorry" I feebly offered didn't make a dent in her pain. I contacted my dad, sisters, and sons to inform them of my transgression so they could be prepared if the media picked up the story and decided to share it with the world.

Denise and I had committed to bringing treats to the home high school football game the night after my release and helping serve the players afterward. Our youngest, Isaac, was starting his senior year. He would take the field with the team that night. After spending the day alone, reflecting in my car in a local park, I mustered up the mental strength to do the walk of shame in front of my community at the football game. I was positive everyone in our town of 9,000 people already knew of my crimes, and they were going to have stones ready to pitch at my head when I showed up.

I brought cookies to the school and tried to crack a smile. One friend, Doug, silently squeezed my shoulder to reassure me I'd survive. Others approached me and said, "Hey, Tim! How's it going?" "Hi, Tim." "Where's Denise?" "Isaac had a good game!"

Wait a minute! I wasn't getting the judgmental stares I expected. I came to the realization that perhaps the universe doesn't revolve around the self-

centered Tim Eggebraaten, and people had their own lives and issues to consider instead of focusing on me.

The people who did know about my arrest offered a supportive handshake or a sentiment of "There, but for the grace of God go I."

I was sure there wasn't another human in the world who felt as crappy about the situation as I did. Nothing anyone could say or do to me would be as brutal as what I was saying and doing to myself. I had heard about "rock bottom," and I understand everyone has their breaking point with addiction and abuse. This was my nadir.

Separating drinking from my music gigs was far more challenging in my head than in reality. What I thought was part of the game was a myth. People didn't hire me to party with them; they asked me to provide a musical soundtrack for their event. After several gigs, I could feel my momentum snowballing. Patrons weren't buying me shots or beer, and non-alcoholic Busch quenched my thirst on a hot day. My fingers were no longer slurring, the day-afters were painless, I lost 20 pounds, my shows improved, and my relationship with Denise had never been better. I did have one guy ask me, "Tim, are you still going to be funny at your shows?" "I'm not sure! You'll have to decide for yourself and let me know," was the only thing I could think of to tell him. Another friend said to me, "Tim, I miss you." "What?!?!? I'm still here! I'm just not drinking!"

August 31, 2017, began the farewell tour of the "Tim Eggebraaten Drunk-Fest" and the dawning of a new age without the crutch of alcohol. I'm thankful my relationship with alcohol didn't reach a point of physical or psychological addiction. I'm not sure what label would apply to the problems I had, but I didn't experience withdrawals or other physical reactions to quitting.

Denise will periodically ask me if I miss drinking or have any temptations to start up again. Absolutely not.

I know I'm no expert on dependency, but there are people all around us who are—and they can help.

The first step for each of us is to recognize we have a problem, own it, and ask for help. It's never easy, but the results can be glorious!

ELEVEN
ROAD TRIPS WITH DAD

When my mom died in July 2016 after a tough battle with cancer, my dad was alone for the first time since they were married on March 12, 1960. For 56 years, they raised four children, squabbled, loved, prayed, traveled, and adored their grandchildren and great-grandchildren. They squeezed out every ounce of the breath they had been given.

A few months after Mom died, Dad was having difficulty breathing and developed a cough he couldn't shake. After multiple trips to specialists, he was ultimately diagnosed with Idiopathic Pulmonary Fibrosis (IPF). "Kenny, there's no known cure for this disease," his doctor said. "We'll give you medications to try to slow the effects, but eventually, your lungs will quit working." Hearing a disheartening prognosis is never easy, but my dad seized the choice of how he would respond. "None of us are getting out of this gig alive!" he often reminded us.

I believe nothing happens by mistake or accident, and I have witnessed countless events reinforcing my confidence. Our journey on earth is peppered with people and events put into our lives for a purpose, meaning that events happen FOR us and not TO us. The timing of the monumental event, Dad's health diagnosis, coincided perfectly with my planned retirement from law enforcement at the end of 2016.

As we celebrated Christmas that year, I told Dad about my one-man band music gigs lined up in southwest Florida and suggested he join me for a road trip. "Tim Bob, I don't want to be a burden," he said.

"Come on, Dad!" reasoned one of my sisters. "Think of the fun you'll have!" My wife and three sisters can be persuasive, and we finally got Dad to agree to ride in the copilot seat with me to Florida. In January, we loaded up the tan Subaru Outback, picked up our friend Ben, hooked up a trailer for my speakers and music gear, and began our quest. Ben is a farmer who took advantage of having more free time in the winter and decided to road trip it with my dad and me. He and his wife, Lisa, are frequent travel partners of Denise and me, and Lisa and Denise opted to fly to Florida and meet us there.

I love driving and drove most of the way. Dad occupied the front passenger seat, and Ben dispensed snacks and daily crop price updates—mostly corn. The GPS was locked and loaded with our destination, Fort Myers Beach. For being 78 years old, my dad was highly tech-savvy. His smartphone worked hard during the 4,885-mile expedition as he scanned Facebook to see what so-and-so had for breakfast and the news to see what President Trump had tweeted the night before. "Well, it looks like Betty made bacon and eggs this morning. Here's a picture. Can you believe what Trump said this time? Should he be saying that as President? Let's see what everybody thinks!"

Dad was king of creeping on social media. He peered into his Facebook friends' pages, dove three or four levels deep into their friends, and learned about people none of us knew. "When women get together for coffee and talk, it's gossip. When men gather, we're sharing facts," he would rationalize, then enlightened Ben and me on the goings-on of a collection of characters.

Periodically, Dad texted my sisters updates to apprise them of our daily progress. Years prior, a cyst on his spine and subsequent surgeries had caused him to lose most of the dexterity in his dominant right hand. He could still playfully flip the occasional bird to friends and family well enough that they understood his meaning. I think he learned that gesture from Mom. Whenever Dad made remarks Mom recognized as questionable, she would adjust her glasses with her middle finger while telling Dad, "Kenneth, fix your glasses."

Dad learned to write left-handed and proficiently spoke his text messages into his smartphone. He could still use his right hand to smash SEND. However, his conversations with the artificial intelligence Siri were cumbersome at best. "Siri, what is the weather forecast for Fort Myers Beach, Florida?" Dad would inquire.

"Go ahead. I'm listening." Siri responded.

"Siri, what…"

"Go ahead. I'm listening."

"Damn it! Siri, what is the fore…"

"I can't quite understand what you're saying."

The back-and-forth between my dad and Siri was better than any entertainment we could dial up on the radio!

Dad sometimes ratted me out to my sisters, "Kris, Timmy put a stinky sock in my face this morning!" "Girls, help me! Timmy ate the last cookie!" Ben seemed to enjoy the banter.

We kept a loose itinerary on the way to Florida. Every two hundred miles, we stopped for fuel, stretched, grabbed a bite to eat, used the facilities, and got back on the road. We never pushed too hard, and when we decided we had enough driving for a day, we fired up Priceline on the phone, rented a hotel room, and called it a day.

As we settled in, our standard operating procedure was to get Dad a glass of ice and pour him "two fingers" of brandy. This meant positioning two fingers together horizontally at the bottom of the glass and filling the drink to the top edge of the tip finger. Occasionally, the fingers got separated, and the portion was two very generous fingers.

The next step was to flip on the Bose Bluetooth speaker and play Tennessee Ernie Ford's "Alleluia" on YouTube. Dad loved that song, making it the first pick every evening on our personalized YouTube concert series. Dad and I listened to music together regularly throughout my adult life.

After a few songs and a good taste of brandy, Dad would say, "Fellas, you're on your own. I'm calling it quits." Ben and I sometimes stayed up, but we usually followed Dad's lead. In the morning, we packed up and hit the trail. "Hurrup! Let's boooook," was a phrase Dad must have heard during his childhood because he laid it on thick to my family as we grew up. He was relatively patient but hated long delays or showing up late.

In addition to enjoying varying landscapes, we had fun detecting different accents as we pressed onward. For example, as we refueled in Indiana, I clearly understood the gas station employees. "Thanks for stopping! Have a great day." A couple of hours later, I detected many y'alls in Kentucky, and we had to listen intently to decipher the message.

In northern Kentucky, I made an executive decision to find a pub that served authentic Kentucky Bourbon. Google suggested a spot just a few miles away. We paused outside Bungalow Joe's Family Grill and Pub in Shelbyville, Kentucky, stopping for the obligatory travel photo. As we entered just after one in the afternoon, I swear a record needle screeched across an album, followed by complete silence as four locals eyeballed us.

The tension eased, and they gave a friendly nod as we bellied up to the bar on our mission to locate and consume a shot of local bourbon. However, when I gave the bartender a loud "howdy," my accent refocused the boys' attention. "How do three travelers get a shot of local bourbon?" I sounded like I had just stepped out of the movie "Fargo," with my "O's" exaggerated, as in "MinnesOta," "bOat," and "mOuntain." Dang it! They know we're Yankees! I slept through history class, so I wasn't sure what side Kentucky folks were on during the Civil War or how they would react to us.

They mumbled to the lone bartender, and she grabbed a Small Batch Bulleit 95 Rye bottle. One of the guys told us it was distilled just a few miles away. So, I ordered a shot with a beer chaser. "Here's to ya, fellas!" we toasted and sipped our drinks as the spectators watched our reactions. I don't know if the bourbon honestly tasted good or if the adventure made it seem better than it was. I thought it was smooth and tasty. Ben and Dad respectfully disagreed. The quartet of onlookers looked relieved and proud as if their uncle concocted it out back in his illegal still. At one point, they all jumped in and talked simultaneously. Their thick dialect made it nearly impossible to understand one alone. When all four chimed in, we just smiled, nodded, and pretended to understand.

As we left Kentucky and entered Tennessee, we made a slight detour to spend the evening at my uncle Norman's house in Seymour, just southeast of Knoxville. Uncle Norm was one of Dad's 12 siblings—seven boys and six girls—and he had recently left Minnesota to live in the Tennessee hills closer to his daughter and grandchildren. We navigated the Outback and trailer through Seymour's narrow streets, missing Norm's house at least three times.

Uncle Norm and Aunt Jeanette welcomed us and offered a quick tour of their home before we visited my cousins and their children. The song "Wagon Wheel" came to life as I saw dogwood flowers for the first time and belted out the lyrics, "Picking me a bouquet of dogwood flowers."

At my cousin's house, dinner, hugs, and conversation carried us through the evening until the little ones pooped out, and we returned to Norm and Jeanette's. My dad, Norm, Ben, and I gathered around the dining room table while Jeanette sensed not much good would come out of the next several hours and went to bed.

The table-top conference began innocently enough. "So, how is your trip so far?" Norm inquired. He then fetched a bucket of ice from the freezer, and Ben grabbed the jug of brandy. Some chose to dilute the nectar with water, but Dad and I stuck with brandy on the rocks. It was a special occasion, and nobody was driving, so bolder three-finger portions replaced the usual two-fingers.

Uncle Norm had sent me a detailed route suggestion from Minnesota based on his vast experience and scolded me about my choices so far in our trek. "You stayed where? How did you get there? Why didn't you stick to the plan?" I apologized and blamed my GPS and our loose itinerary.

We roamed over a lot of territory in those hours. "How are the kids?" "Ben, tell us about yourself." "When I was stationed in Germany…" We laughed, reminisced, cried about lost loved ones, and dreamed about the future. While solving most of the world's problems, we drained one jug and sent Ben on a mission to locate a suitable replacement in the car. We created a lifetime of memories that night. Unforgettable!

We found our way to our sleeping quarters. I took the recliner, Ben flopped on the couch, and Dad and Norm secured actual beds. I'm sure Jeanette was impressed with our ability to successfully address pressing global issues and grow even more intelligent, taller, and better-looking. Ben had educated us about the hidden fact that "Brandy is what wine wants to be when it grows up." We were not aware of that hidden fact.

We were in no hurry the following day to get back on the road, so we stopped by a local diner for an incredible break from our overnight fast: Bacon, eggs, juice, coffee—the works. When good people surround you, and you have the time of your life, the food somehow even tastes better. I privately coerced the waitress into letting me take care of our tab, only to raise my uncle's ire again.

Southwest Florida didn't disappoint. The warm vitamin D worked magic on our pasty white Minnesota skin, and we felt our batteries recharge. Ben and I picked up our wives at the airport so they could join in the fun. We shared tales of the road with them, like kids relating their summer camp experience with their parents, intentionally leaving out specific details. The Florida experience ended with all of us safely home, hundreds of photos, and a permanent smile when we reflected on that week.

Dad's health was slowly deteriorating, but more travels were still to come. As the days passed, a lifetime of lessons from my dad began to sink in.

TWELVE
FILTER THE STATIC

In March 2017, Dad and I again loaded up the Outback and set sail for Mesa, Arizona, with a way-out-of-the-way stop in Ontario, Oregon, to play music and see friends. We traveled sans Ben this time, who opted to fly to Arizona and meet up with us. I again had gigs scheduled, and we rented the same trailer to haul my equipment. We were getting good at our road trip routine, with stops every couple of hours and no bickering over who would pay for the fuel. Even my dad's tattling to my sisters was less frequent.

Each portion of the country exhibited unique beauty. From the plains to the mountains, it was all incredible. Dad was like a kid whenever we saw a train, proof that his 40 years with the railroad had indelibly marked his soul. He proudly waved at nearly every train and hollered, "Thank you, fellas! Keep working to fund my retirement!" As the mountains of Montana came into view, he let out a high-pitched "Whee!" as if it were the first time he had seen them.

The decline in my dad's health between our Florida trip in January and the Arizona trip in March was noticeable, with his oxygen tank graduating from "I should use it" to "I need to use it."

The machine's constant purr as it regenerated usable oxygen became part of the background noise. Dad started chapping under his nose and, without luck, tried various ointments to keep it at bay. My Superman was physically withering before me, but his sense of humor and steadfast positive attitude somehow grew exponentially with each diminished breath.

Friends in Oregon had put together a little bash at a place called George Yasuda's Bar. Live music ended in a spirited jam session, drinks, and laughter alongside an incredible handmade wood bar with gorgeous craftsmanship. My friends made my dad feel like a newly returned war hero who had singlehandedly saved 79 schoolchildren and three nuns from an active volcano.

When Dad and I got to Mesa, we stayed in a hotel before moving to our rented condo. It was one more hotel, another brandy nightcap, more Tennessee Ernie Ford, and Dad's oft-repeated, "Booger, I'm so proud of you! Love ya, man!"

"Booger" (with an emphasis on the BOO) was one of the first nicknames my dad gave me. I don't remember its origin, but in my adulthood, our phone calls always started with my saying, "POOH-pah, you dirty dog!" He replied, "BOO-ger, you rascal!" I never questioned if Dad loved me because he told me almost daily that he was proud of me. I can't think of a more positive phrase to tell someone. Even when I was in elementary school, and he worked the night shift, Dad told me he loved me as he headed for bed and I was heading out the door to school. What a boost to start the day.

Dad's younger brother from California, Ray, came to Arizona to stay for a few days. The two aging men talked about their past and future. Dad told Ray, "I wonder how it will be when I die. Pat's death seemed painless. Will I suffocate? I hope it's not painful." It was remarkable listening to him contemplate his impending death. We all know we'll die at some time, but his finish line was more evident than ours.

In July 2017, Dad and I flew to Las Vegas and spent four days—10 hours a day—listening to barbershop choruses and quartets from around the world. It was a marathon of harmony that would kill some people, but we loved it. Uncle Ray again arrived from California, and the three of us sang barbershop tags in our room and listened to world-class harmonies from thousands of singers in the hallways, elevators, casinos, and lobbies. The harmonies struck me because they reminded me of life. It's a challenge to get all the parts of our lives in harmony, and when one part is off, the whole shebang struggles. Even if fleeting, the feeling is stunning when the harmonies are tight!

Through a lifetime of examples capped off by our road trips, my dad's attitude is embedded in my brain. Every morning, he awoke struggling to breathe. Yet he got dressed and humbly slid into his wheelchair to be pushed to the car. He hated asking for help, but his deteriorating health left him no choice. After settling him into his front seat copilot position, we would plug his oxygen machine into the cigarette lighter and enter our coordinates into the GPS. My dad would smack his hand on the dashboard and say, "Timbob! I wonder what today's adventures will be!" The man had 78 years of refusing to focus on the negatives in life.

On November 28, 2017, just two and a half months before his death, Dad called me to wish me a happy 51st birthday. I couldn't get to the phone. As I listened to his rendition of "Happy Birthday" on the recording, I thought, *Dude, your starting pitch is way too high! You'll never make it in that key!* Sure enough, he had to adjust midstream to a lower key to fit his voice. He wrapped up his performance with, "I love you so much, and I'm so proud of you! Buh bye!" It was the last voice message Dad left me, and I have never been so thankful to have missed a call because I will have this voicemail forever. The disease was taking his breath, strength, and much of his weight, but it couldn't touch his undeniable attitude.

Dad avoided moving to a senior living facility and remained home. My three sisters and I teamed with our families to ensure Dad had somebody checking in with him regularly and then, as his needs increased, staying with him around the clock. As he grew weaker, we had to help him stand up, and simple tasks like urinating now required aid. One morning, my sister Wendy and I helped Dad get out of bed to pee. Discomfort all around. Nobody would have blamed Dad for lamenting his physical deficiencies and the fact that his oldest and youngest children had to hold him up to pee into a handheld plastic urinal. Instead, as Dad was urinating, his body hunched over like a capital C, he looked out the window of his bedroom and said, "Huh! Would you look at that sunrise? It's going to be a beautiful day!"

As I travel the country sharing music and stories, I meet people with their own compelling stories. I didn't have a choice about being born a white male in 1966 to two loving parents in northwest Minnesota. As I get to know folks who had grown up without knowing their dad or whose father was a mean alcoholic who vented their frustrations on their children, I'm even more thankful for my childhood. My mom and dad's contagious positivity taught me to always look for an upside to any situation, and they helped to hardwire my brain to see the good around me.

I'm not suggesting the secret to living an enriched life is as simple as *choosing* to be happy. We all have times when our rhythm of life pounds out the "oom-pa-pa" of a polka while we clumsily try to dance the Macarena. My parents modeled how to keep recognizing the beauty around us. Their technique allowed me to thrive mentally, physically, and spiritually in a law enforcement career that dripped with toxic negativity. These same tactics will also help you.

As Dad's health diminished, I noticed the magnitude of his positivity. It was another dimension of his mindset. I watched my dad continually, energetically, relentlessly filter the static around him—whether it was people, events, a downturn in his capabilities, or anything else that would drag him down.

We all face daily temptations to fixate on the negative things around us. Social media, traditional media, our friends, families, and co-workers can all feed us bottomless negativity if we choose to let them.

The gas tank cap was always on Dad's side during our road trips. When we stopped for gas, I would activate the latch on the floor on my side to unlock the fuel door. Invariably, Dad would swing his door open and bounce it into the concrete barrier protecting the pumps. How I positioned the car never mattered. He somehow managed to introduce the door to the immovable concrete painfully. Every time, I winced. At first, he apologized, but after multiple incidents, we both became numb to the clank of the door on the concrete.

How could I blame him? Dad's tall frame fit his seat just fine, but he didn't bend well due to fake knees and hips and a spine with little flexibility. I was blessed to inherit many of these traits, and my friend Mike affectionately calls my dad and me "uni-back" due to our inability to bend. Add to that dad's weakened right hand, and he was going to bang the heck out of the door. I could choose to get upset. Or learn to see things differently.

For years, I had difficulty grasping why my mom refused to wipe the greasy fingerprints off the long mirror at the end of the hallway in the house where I grew up. At some point, one of their grandkids probably wiped their snotty nose and put their grimy hands on the mirror while looking at their reflection. A shot of

Windex and a paper towel would have quickly eliminated the smear, but Mom rejected cleaning that part of the mirror.

Mom was never obsessed with a clean, organized house. She wasn't a slob, but an orderly home wasn't at the top of her priorities. Still, it perplexed me why she let those fingerprints remain.

"Mom, why don't you ever wipe off the mirror?" I asked. Her gentle smile was the only response I would receive.

Then, one day, I finally understood why Mom cherished those greasy fingerprints. I opened the passenger side door of our tan Subaru Outback for Denise and noticed the craters in the door. I smiled. The pockmarked door reminds me of my dad and the incredible road trips we shared. Scars, nicks, dents, and greasy fingerprints are excellent reminders of a well-lived life.

THIRTEEN
LETTER WRITING

As I listened to Dad tell the home hospice social worker about the powerful effects of a letter he received from a family friend, my eyes filled with tears. "This letter makes me feel better than the morphine I'm on!" Dad's time on earth was running out, and my sisters and I had requested hospice care to help make him comfortable during his final days.

My dad had made a difference in the lives of countless people. He was honest, dependable, firm, and fair. People easily related to him and readily called him "friend." As child number 11 of 13 children born to Arthur and Helga (Andreson) Eggebraaten, baby Kenny grew to be the tallest of the bunch, making even his siblings smile.

For nearly two years, in his mid-70s, my dad suffered from incurable Idiopathic Pulmonary Fibrosis (IPF). He accepted his fate and prepared for his next journey—to heaven.

In late 2017, our friend Dr. Julie Larson wrote Dad a letter. Julie had attended a conference for medical professionals where a speaker highlighted the powerful effects of writing notes of gratitude to people who have inspired them. The research compared the impact on the letter writer to the calming effects of Prozac.

Moreover, the recipient experienced similar outcomes! Julie's letter to Dad was short but packed a punch. The handwritten message told my dad why Julie thought he was so special. She noted specific characteristics in my dad that inspired her to be a better person, like his ability to listen to others actively, his wonderful sense of humor, and the great feeling people felt from just being around him.

Dad was at our house in Detroit Lakes when Julie delivered the letter just a few months before he passed away. He was in constant pain, struggling to breathe, and growing steadily weaker, yet he still wanted to come to Detroit Lakes to watch our youngest son, Isaac, perform in his school's staging of "High School Musical."

The impact of Julie's words on Dad also touched us as he read them aloud. I helped him snap a smartphone photo of the note to keep it with him constantly. Powerful stuff! He carefully positioned that letter and its blue envelope on his home office desk, front, and center, amid other vital documents. When he talked with visitors, I would fetch the letter for him, and he always said its words were more potent than any drug a doctor could give him. Today, that letter resides in my home office and continues to have a positive ripple effect worldwide through social media and speaking engagements.

This tactic of writing a significant, heartfelt, affirming letter to someone who has inspired you has astounding benefits.

Steve Toepfer at Kent State University at Salem in Ohio found that writing letters of gratitude measurably improved personal well-being in three areas: happiness, life satisfaction, and depression. His study required that the letters written by test subjects couldn't be trivial, in other words, more than a thanks for a gift or a note "saying hello." Writing about something important made all the difference. Toepfer found that writing a letter weekly for three weeks boosted positive benefits even more. This is a powerful tool to increase well-being for us and others.

Dr. Martin Seligman has also researched gratitude and its relationship with authentic happiness. Widely considered the "Father of Positive Psychology," Seligman takes the practice of gratitude letter writing one step further and suggests the writer meet with the recipient and read the letter to that person. It's an even more powerful way to tell someone they inspire you.

The evidence is clear that the recipient, sender, and people who hear about the letter all experience positive physiological responses, an uplift akin to Prozac and other medications used to treat mild depression. In addition to feeling physically better, we reap mental and spiritual benefits.

In his book *The Sender*, Dr. Kevin Elko writes about a football coach going through cancer treatments who received daily anonymous letters that lifted him up and slowly changed his attitude. The book demonstrates the life-changing results of a simple act.

Who has made a difference in your life? Think of someone, living or dead, who helped you get where you are. Take a few minutes today and write that person a letter. Tell them why they are essential to you. Texts or emails also work, but there's some extra power in a handwritten note. Send them your letter, and you will be amazed at the feeling of "Return to Sender" you get back. Even if the person you write to is no longer living, write that letter and keep it as a reminder to yourself.

This activity is simple but not easy. It's simple because it doesn't cost much money or take much time, and we all have people who pop to mind who have made a difference in our lives. It's certainly not easy, though, because sharing our feelings might be a leap for us. Like anything else that isn't easy initially, our capacity for this task improves with practice.

Why not begin with a list of six people who have inspired you—perhaps a teacher, coach, parent, sibling, friend, or mentor? Commit to writing a pen-and-paper letter each week for six weeks. What effect will that new habit have on you? Before your impulse to follow through fades, start now by taking a moment to make that list of six people.

After sharing this exercise with people around the country, I sometimes receive messages from attendees about the outcomes they experienced. A high school principal, for example, wrote a letter to his mother, who had died several years ago. He knew she would never read the letter, but the act of letter writing still profoundly impacted him.

Whatever we have encountered in life, we can all find reasons to be grateful.

My dad continued his positive impact on us until the very end—and beyond. On February 13, 2018, Kenneth Gerhardt Eggebraaten died peacefully at home.

My three sisters and I sang with my dad the previous evening, laughed, and told stories. If someone had spied us through the window, they would have thought we were having an old-fashioned hootenanny! We all went to bed after Dad had his morphine and a bite of banana.

I was in the bedroom across the narrow hallway from his room, with a baby monitor cranked up in case Dad needed anything during the night. "Nurse!" he often shouted, with one of us rushing to his aid. Dad had an incredible sense of humor, even in his final days. He was constantly filtering the static and focusing on the positive.

I could hear the now-familiar purr of the oxygen machine that methodically purred and *pssshhhh*-ed as it produced life-sustaining oxygen. I could also hear my father breathing comfortably. I was startled awake around 5 am and went into Dad's room. Dad was lying in bed, glasses still on, hands on his chest, a half-eaten banana on the bedstand, and a comfortable look on his face. I quietly approached him with a combination of not wanting to startle him and wanting to see if he was still alive. With decades of law enforcement experience, I have seen many deceased people, so I was glad it was me checking on Dad instead of one of my sisters. I felt his wrist for a pulse and found none. He was still warm to the touch, so I knew it hadn't been very long since he had passed away.

Why did I wake up suddenly? Was it a sound? A lack of sound? Or maybe something in the spiritual realm gently nudged me awake that morning to let me know Dad's life as we knew it had ended and another had begun. I had a similar experience after my brother-from-another-mother Chad Jutz died. He peacefully appeared at the foot of my bed, and I said, "I love you, brother!" He smiled and said, "I know. I love you, too!" I don't pretend to know how any of these things happen. Maybe they can be explained by exhaustion or psychological trauma. I believe, however, beyond any shadow of a doubt, that the spirits of Chad and my dad visited me and that we will be reunited someday!

FOURTEEN
REGAINING MY RHYTHM

I n my early police officer days, Stormin' Norman entered my life to help me recognize my life's rhythm was off-beat. If I didn't do something about it, I would become one of those statistical burnouts we all hear about—or maybe we feel like we're already there. My encounter with Norman began a long journey of learning to deliberately focus on my attitude and apply proven tactics to regain my rhythm.

Practicing those tactics allows them to become habits. I don't mean we should mindlessly pretend everything is sunshine and lollipops—because it isn't. Our goal should be to deal with life's challenges while remembering the uniquely precious gift of each moment.

Most circumstances in life are beyond our control. Like the driver putzing in the passing lane for 37 miles and refusing to let you by. Or the arrival of brutal Minnesota winters. Or ugly rumors flying around the community about us. In fact, we have little influence over so many aspects of our lives. However, our reactions and attitudes toward these events are entirely within our control. We grow better at responding through diligent practice.

Since I retired from active police work, mindfulness and meditation have become increasingly important to keeping my life pounding with a steady rhythm.

When we are mindful—that is, when we acknowledge and appreciate the present while not worrying about the past or the future—we train our brains to recognize the beauty around us. Being stuck in traffic becomes less of "Oh, poor me! These idiots don't have a clue what they're doing!" and more of "I'm PART of the traffic! These people are likely after the same things I want—love, a sense of belonging, and peace." We begin to see beauty when we strip away powerful emotions and view the world with thankfulness instead of contempt.

A couple of years after the police chiefs retreat, where I first encountered the concept of mindfulness, one of my nieces, Jordan Wavra, happened to be recording several videos delving into the topic. Her target market was young women, especially mothers, but I knew I needed them too. Jordan kindly extended a friends-and-family discount to me, so I downloaded her complete video series and continued to grow in the experience of living in the moment.

I have since subscribed to two guided meditation apps, Headspace and Waking Up. As my practice has become more consistent, I have become increasingly less anxious and, light years later, less reactive to stressful situations. Even a recent trip to Los Angeles, spending four hours in LAX waiting for my rental car and then driving on the 87 lanes of Interstate 405 with 18.3 million cars whizzing by me, allowed me an extreme test of how far I have come due to meditation. It was a breeze! A few years ago, I would have screamed profanities, flipped off dozens of idiot drivers, and destroyed the car horn.

I recently flew from Arizona back home to Minnesota. Everything amazed me; it was as if I was seeing and experiencing it all for the first time. The mesmerizing flow of vehicles to the airport, lines of people weaving through security checkpoints, maintenance crews cleaning the airport, restaurant employees serving hungry and thirsty travelers, workers with orange vests and wands sending hand signals to pilots, the choreography of planes on the tarmac. I'm sure the hundreds of people on my plane weren't seeing the world as I was. But there was so much to observe. A flight delay became an opportunity to watch the airline employees skillfully scramble to find passengers alternate flights and get their luggage to their chosen destination. With keen eyes, it felt like nothing short of a miracle!

Life will always be full of challenges, but mindfulness means we can accept, deal with, or entirely dismiss those concerns. Their true importance has been exposed, and we can chuck them where they belong, a bucket labeled "not really a big deal."

With this mindfulness mindset, when I play guitar and entertain others, I become keenly aware of the "now." It's made me even closer and more impactful to my audience as I focus on reaching them with my music and message. My concentration has become so attuned that the vibration of my guitar strings seems to slow as I observe each string emanate sound. Song lyrics resonate afresh as I pay attention to their meaning and their possible connecting points with listeners.

For most of my adult life, I used my power of focus for cop concerns. Now, mindfulness and meditation help me see a bigger world. Things went unnoticed before. I now marvel at the beauty all around me.

It was a few weeks before my 55th birthday, and I had been practicing mindfulness and appreciating my surroundings for a year. Our winter vacation had been phenomenal, absorbing the people and stunning surroundings of Cabo San Lucas, Mexico. My phone alarm buzzed just past five a.m. on the fourth day of our adventure, but I didn't need an alarm. I was already awake, antici-pating chasing yet another stunning sunrise. The coffee maker auto-timer had fired up on cue, and the steaming black gold was ready to jump-start my brain and heart.

As Denise and our crew of friends navigated toward our pre-determined viewing deck, the eastern sky was already aglow in ma-jestic purples and pinks mixed with wispy clouds and a cerulean sky. Google informed us this time of day—before actual sunrise—was called "nautical dawn." When I paid attention, I found the air was full of the sound of water lapping the shore, the monotonous hum of HVAC compressors, the distant horn of a passing cruise ship, and the conversations of my travel partners.

I overflowed with appreciation for another opportunity to ob-serve this far-south sunrise. It meant we were still alive and "on the right side of the grass," as old-timers say, and we had lived long enough to take in the glory of a new day dawning. I stood away from the others, who were marveling aloud at the unbelievable sky and its glory and plotting the activities of the day.

As I silently took it all in and thanked God for another shot at living, I spotted a figure on the beach, silhouetted in the morning light.

At first glance, I couldn't determine what it was, maybe a gar-bage bag on the beach, but as the sky grew brighter and further illuminated the sand, I could see the outlines of a person. He lay curled up on the beach with a guitar by his head! My curiosity was piqued, and I asked my son, Luke, "How cool would it be to play guitar on a Mexican beach during a magnificent sunrise?" As the words came out of my mouth, my body gravitated toward the steps leading to the beach. As I got closer, I saw the man was barefoot. He used his jacket as a blanket and his black acoustic guitar as a pillow.

His eyes opened beneath cracked and bent sunglasses, and I said in my best Spanish, learned in two college quarters and ten days in Spain, "Amigo! La Guitarra?" He smiled and handed me his guitar. A sticker on the body of the guitar said, "Kenneth." My father-in-law *and* my dad were both named Kenneth! A sign from them, maybe? "Qual es su nombre?" I asked. "Joe Commish" was his response. "Mi nombre es Tim. Mucho gusto, Joe Commish!"

I expected this caseless guitar to be unplayable, way off-key, and need fresh strings. Amazingly, the axe was perfectly tuned! The intoxicating sunrise and beach scene may have affected my tonal perception, but the guitar sounded magical. I started in the key of G and began stringing together all the Spanish words I could muster to create an original song for Joe and some onlookers waiting for the sunrise. Words like "playa," "agua," "Joe Commish," "guitarra," "bonita," and other phrases made zero sense in the order I plugged them in.

The result was an original tune destined to be the most excellent song Joe and I had ever written on a beach on the Gulf of Mexico in November! Joe even crooned a few bars once the melody became obvious. After my musical interpolation, Joe was up to bat. He grabbed his guitar and muttered a few Spanish phrases, and his dirty fingers and untrimmed nails danced along the neck of that weathered six-string.

Mi amigo nuevo had everything going on with that guitar—harmonics, rhythm, lead licks, and a few hammer-ons. He covered the expanse of the guitar's neck with chapped hands that hadn't seen soap and water for days. Then Joe sang out in a powerful voice most live music venues would gladly pay for to serenade their patrons.

We traded the guitar back and forth and soaked in the sunrise. Before we parted ways, I gave him a challenge coin, one of the custom coins that carry my mom's mantra of "I Am, I Can, I

WILL!" I created the metal token to keep her legacy alive. Joe's smile showed me he understood the explanation, even with my curbed abilities to speak his native tongue.

We shook hands, and I snapped a quick photo of us before we parted. It wasn't until the next day that I looked at the picture and saw the image of two men from vastly different backgrounds united by a sunrise, marking a day with endless possibilities for both, regardless of their paths. The humanity we shared that morning dwarfed any of our differences. Rock on, a mi hermano! Vaya con Dios!

As each of us searches for our rhythm of life, we must quiet our minds and notice the Joe Commishes along our path.

We can get caught up in assumptions about others based on appearance. We really know little unless we take time to ask questions, actively listen, interact, and mindfully appreciate them as individuals.

FIFTEEN
TAKE YOUR SHOT

I was playing a music gig at the Detroit Lakes Holiday Inn to an audience composed chiefly of building contractors and construction sales reps. I was leaning into my standard set when a big, burly fella struck a stance in front of my stage. He stared at me. I eyed him without staring back. Judging by his paws, he had swung a hammer most of his life.

As I finished my song set, he approached the stage and extended his vice-grip of a hand to shake my hand. I reached out and put my right hand into his death grip. He squeezed tightly, pulled me close, and told me, "I hate cops!"

My stage setup doesn't contain anything super effective for self-defense, and I wasn't about to bludgeon him with my baby—my guitar. I asked, "Well, where do we go from here?" He said, "Man, I wished I could play guitar, and man, the songs you play are awesome!"

I was relieved my new cop-hater friend wasn't going to kill me and dance on stage with my body as his trophy. As we chatted, he again expressed his wish to play guitar. I told him I wished I could build things. He couldn't grasp that someone couldn't make something as simple as a doghouse. He clearly overestimated my ability to construct things from wood.

I told him I had once asked Ron, the man who built my house, for plans to construct a doghouse. Ron told me to "just build one!" I told him that I would need parts prepared and labeled, with detailed instructions to attach side A to side B using screw C. Apparently, the world needs to know that while I can make up songs on the fly and have other specific abilities, construction trades isn't on that list.

My friend Lisa can look at a piece of land and visualize what kind of house would go on that property, where it will sit, how the roof line will match the surroundings, and what type of dog will play in the yard. She can draw it up and build it into a beautiful home. I look at the same land and see just land.

Similarly, my wife, Denise, has an uncanny ability to find the perfect gifts for friends and family, often buying items months before giving them away. I'm amazed at how she can match the receiver's personality with a present. Her gift-giving ability is undoubtedly itself a gift.

My gift is music combined with speaking rolled into entertainment. Music is so much a part of me that some song is almost always running in my head on an old-school record player, the kind with a stack of vinyl poised above the turntable, just waiting for the needle to retreat so it can drop the next record.

A few months after I retired from policing and shifted gears to begin speaking professionally, my eyes snapped open at 2:30 a.m. as the song "My Shot" from the Broadway Musical "Hamilton" blared in my head like a rock concert speaker tower pinned to a make-your-ears-bleed volume.

The sound in my head was so clear I worried it would wake Denise. I got out of bed, my bare feet shuffling on the floor during the 17-step commute to my home office. I went to work editing my keynote presentation under the light of a single desk lamp with "Hamilton" still providing the soundtrack.

I know my gift. I'm ready to use it. And I never know when someone needs the best I can offer.

A couple of summers ago, I learned my friend Billy's health was declining rapidly. I first met Billy more than thirty years earlier when I was a correctional officer, and he was a Moorhead police officer. I got to know him better during our time on a Fishing Derby Committee with the Northwest Minnesota Fraternal Order of Police Lodge 8.

Billy had been diagnosed with dementia, and when his wife died by suicide, Billy's dementia accelerated rapidly, along with his physical health. I had heard he was in a memory care facility in Fargo and planned to stop to see him when I had a music gig nearby. "Don't be surprised if he doesn't recognize you, Tim," warned one of Billy's closest friends. "He didn't even recognize ME! It's so sad to see him like this."

I tried to prepare myself mentally as I wandered the halls of the memory care unit, looking for Billy's room. A staff member directed me to Billy's wing, and I cautiously and optimistically continued searching for Billy. I found him in a dining area. I wasn't sure if he even recognized me as I walked closer. He mumbled a few words and walked toward me. I set down my guitar case and went in for a hug. Plainly, that's what he was mumbling about with his arms outstretched. As I got close enough to embrace my friend, I immediately found out he did NOT want a hug, and I was making him badly agitated. I retreated and tried whispering to calm him.

Billy continued mumbling, and I couldn't understand anything he said. I asked him if I could play him a couple of songs. As I plopped my guitar case on the table, Billy looked at me. The fog in his eyes vanished, and as plainly as I heard him speak when I met him decades earlier, Billy said, "You've been doing this a long time, haven't you, Tim?" I wanted to grab him and say, "Stay with me, Billy! Keep that focus!" As quickly as his brain lit up, it went out again, and he continued speaking nonsensically. It wasn't until I played Jimmy Buffett's "Margaritaville" that the light flickered on momentarily as he lip-synced along with the song.

Billy died a few weeks later. I'm so glad that I had the opportunity to share that moment with my friend. It's the memory of Billy I continue to carry with me.

I was born with rhythm. I lost it. But I have genuinely found it again. I believe I'm living as the person I was meant to be.

Friend, what does the rhythm in your life feel like? Where does it come from? Does the collection of beats arise from the people you spend time with—your family, friends, co-workers, or peers? Do you find it in an activity that gives you an adrenaline rush? Maybe watching your favorite sports team enter the arena to take on their biggest rival? Or perhaps communing with nature on a solo stroll through the woods gets you into your rhythm? How about meditation and focusing on being truly present? Having drinks with friends at your favorite watering hole? Or a deep conversation with a trusted friend? Holding hands with a loved one as you offer comfort and aid during a challenging time?

Our definition of rhythm is unique to each of us, as is the source of that rhythm. But I have a sense that our most robust rhythm often involves using our gifts for the good of people around us. If we're looking to find our beat, it's a tactic that wins every time.

We have all been given gifts. The older I get, the more I recognize this truth and appreciate it even more. Gifts are meant for sharing, which can reward the giver more than the receiver.

Our daily challenge is to lean into the fact that each of us possesses gifts that make us unique. If we all had the same talent, the world would be boring. The world is impoverished and hopeless if we fail to use our different gifts.

Make time today to reflect and recognize the gifts and talents that you have been given. Once you identify your gifts, please don't keep them to yourself. Get out and share them with those who need them. You will discover how good it feels to live in the fullest expression of rhythm and harmony. And the course of your life will be remade by using your gifts. "I Am, I Can, I WILL!"

Now is your moment. Take your shot!
You Are, You Can, You WILL!
Be the Norman!

Family!

RESOURCES

If you feel alone and confused, there are caring, trained individuals and organizations waiting to help. Please know you are NOT alone! We need you! Here are some resources to help you find your rhythm:

Suicide and Crisis Hotline (United States), Call: 988
   Website: https://988lifeline.org/
   Alcoholics Anonymous: https://www.aa.org/

Mindfulness and meditation apps:
These are a few apps I have used to help me explore and practice mindfulness and meditation. Some are free to use, and some have subscription fees. You can find them on their websites or by searching for them in the app store for your mobile device. New apps are constantly in development. I recommend checking them out. The critical piece with any of these apps is to develop a daily habit of using them. Commit to ten minutes a day for 30 days to start!

Mindfulness and Meditation:
   Headspace: www.headspace.com
   Waking Up: www.wakingup.com

Again, the critical piece with any of these apps is to develop a daily habit of using them.

Gratitude Apps:
    3 Good Things
    Gratitude
    Day One Journal

ACKNOWLEDGMENTS

First and foremost, I thank God for the gift of life and the opportunities to share stories, music, and experiences to hopefully make a positive difference and leave my fingerprints on this world. As long as there is breath in this body of mine, I will continue helping others find their beat!

Mom and Dad. For helping shape my love and compassion for others. You were living examples of how to care for others and find beauty in a sometimes ugly world!

Denise. I fell for you the moment I first saw you when we were teenagers so many years ago. You are my soulmate, business partner, travel buddy, and confidante. You are an incredible mother, friend, sister, wife, and daughter. I appreciate your support through the sleepless nights when I was a police officer and as we continue this amazing adventure together. I love you so much!

Joshua, Lucas, and Isaac. My eyes are leaking as I write this. You three men continue to amaze me. Each of you is an incredible blend of smartness (thanks to Denise), love, compassion, entrepreneurial spirit, ingenuity, and tenacity. I am beyond proud of you all and love you more than you can imagine!

Mariah, Olivia, and Kyra. Holy smokes. There is no way I could search the world and find more beautiful, intelligent, tough, motivated, and loving women to walk with my sons on their journey. Witnessing how you interact with those men with honesty, openness, and love is awe-inspiring. I'm so happy you are in our lives. I love you all!

Wendy, Kristen, and Stacey. You three are phenomenal sisters. Thank you for your guidance as we grew up and for your love and support today. I love you!

My law enforcement family. You will always be my brothers and sisters. Thank you for having my back through some crazy situations. Please know I have your six when I see you on the street. If you need anything, know I am here!

Reneé Rongen. Coach! You helped me find my voice as I ventured into the world of professional speaking. You are the guru, my friend, and my mentor. Thank you for encouraging me to be vulnerable and to go deep with my audience by sharing my experiences. I look forward to continuing to grow our friendship!

Kevin Johnson. You helped make this book a reality. Thank you for your work as a book coach, editor, and friend. I'm thankful we were introduced to each other!

Ann Aubitz. Thank you for making the printing process easy, fun, and exciting. I appreciate your patience with this first-time author!

You, the reader. I hope you take the stories in this book and relate them to your life. The message has never been about me but about those who receive it. Thank you so much for being open to learning about your rhythm of life and how to regain and retain that beat. You are a critical component of this world's rhythm section!

ABOUT THE AUTHOR

Tim Eggebraaten, with nearly 28 years in the Criminal Justice field, brings a wealth of experience to his role as a captivating national speaker. From his beginnings as a correctional officer in 1989 to his tenure as Chief of Police, Tim's journey is a testament to his expertise in "working the beat."

Retiring from law enforcement in 2016, Tim embraced the title of "Off Duty Chief," passionately taking his message, music, and talent to the streets. His compelling storytelling and witty perspective on balance, growth, leadership, and life make him a sought-after keynote speaker on the national stage.

Tim's unique approach combines his love for music with his motivational message, taking audiences on an emotional roller coaster. From light-hearted anecdotes to profound insights on loss and mental health, Tim engages and inspires.

Based in Detroit Lakes, Minnesota, Tim shares his life with his wife, Denise, relishing the outdoors, friendships, and family moments with their adult children and two grandsons.

Contact Tim Eggebraaten to bring his inspiring message and music to your organization:

Phone: (218) 325-0224
Email: tim@offdutychief.com
Website: https://www.offdutychief.com

Discover your rhythm of life through Tim's unique perspective and powerful storytelling.